100
of the
WORST
IDEAS
in
HISTORY

**Humanity's Thundering
Brainstorms Turned
Blundering Brain Farts**

MICHAEL N. SMITH AND ERIC KASUM

 sourcebooks

Published by Sourcebooks, Inc.
P.O. Box 4410, Naperville, Illinois 60567-4410
(630) 961-3900
Fax: (630) 961-2168
www.sourcebooks.com

Library of Congress Cataloging-in-Publication Data

Smith, Michael N.
  100 of the worst ideas in history : humanity's thundering brainstorms turned blundering brain farts / by Michael N. Smith and Eric Kasum.
       pages cm
  Includes bibliographical references.
  (trade : alk. paper) 1. World history—Humor. 2. World history—Anecdotes. 3. History—Miscellanea. I. Kasum, Eric. II. Title. III. Title: One hundred of the worst ideas in history.
  D23.5.S65 2014
  909—dc23

2013048227

Printed and bound in the United States of America.

POD 10 9 8 7 6 5 4 3

To Phyllis, who helped me become a better writer.
To Walt, who helped me become a better worker.
To Debora and Drew, who helped me become a
better person.—Mike

To Marah, my angel and the light of my life.
To Ben and John, the most wonderful sons in the
whole world, you make me so proud. And to my dad,
Michael, who gave me my writing dream.—Eric

CONTENTS

INTRODUCTION

WHAT WERE THEY THINKING?

They are priceless, multifaceted jewels of misjudgment. Masterworks of the moronic. Steroid-juiced stupidity wearing a size 9XX dunce cap embroidered with one simple word: "Duh."

They are the colossally, cringingly, often laughably bad notions that have leapt from the short-circuiting synapses of some of the world's brightest (and dimmest) brains, now faithfully chronicled here as *100 of the Worst Ideas in History*.

Hailing from the worlds of politics, popular culture, international relations, finance, business, sports, entertainment, and news—from the near and distant past—these shoddy concepts have started wars, sunk countries, wrecked companies, scuttled careers, lost millions, endangered Earth, and left the bad idea's mommy or daddy as red faced as, well, *your* mom or dad will be when they learn that you like to dress your pit bull as one of the Backstreet Boys.

On this rollicking romp through the bungles and stumbles of humanity, we'll:

★ Meet the U.S. president who starts each day skinny-dipping in the Potomac.
★ Sample the "dental hygiene product" that could rot your teeth.
★ Get an earful of the hit singing group that can't really sing.
★ Munch on the tasty new snack food that might just give you diarrhea.
★ Drop by the restaurant chain named after a derogatory term for African Americans.
★ Encounter the famed archaeologist whose discovery of the "missing link" is revealed to be a monkey jaw glued to a human skull.
★ Stick an angry ferret down our pants for fun and prizes.
★ Plus so much more (of so much less).

Peppered with scores of info-taining photos, "Hey-I-Didn't-Know-That" factoids, and perspective-gaining "Afterthoughts," this collection of our species' most stupendously stinky thinking spotlights how the ideas of yesterday—from funny flubs to the stunningly strange to classic mind-bogglers—continue to resonate in each of our lives today.

Without further ado and in no particular order, here are 100 of history's thundering brainstorms that turned out to be blundering brain farts.

WHOPPING HISTORICAL FOUL-UPS & FAUX PAS

The President's
SCANDALOUS
EM-BARE-ASS-MENT

the BAD IDEA:

Start each day with a skinny-dip in the Potomac.

the genius BEHIND IT: U.S. president John Quincy Adams

the brainstorm STRUCK: 1825

MICHAEL N. SMITH AND ERIC KASUM

Nearly a half century after George Washington dons a three-cornered hat, courageously crosses the Delaware River, and defeats the British redcoats, President John Quincy Adams strips down to his birthday suit, swims naked in the Potomac River, and leaves America red faced.

Giving "crack of dawn" a whole new meaning, each morning Adams sneaks down to the riverbank, surreptitiously undresses, and proceeds to folly about with the local ducks and geese—all the while naked as a jaybird.

**from bad
TO WORSE:**

Reporter Anne Royall, upon learning of Adams's au naturel aquatic adventures, hides out in the Potomac's foliage and catches the unsuspecting Prez in the buff. Opportunistically scooping up the commander in chief's briefs, she holds his clothing captive until Adams reluctantly agrees to grant her a long-awaited interview.

Although the interview goes swimmingly—and Royall promises to keep the president's daily skinny-dip a watertight secret—other reporters eventually learn about Adams's ballsy escapades and expose him (so to speak), much to his (and the nation's) embarrassment.

**dumb
LUCK:**

The exposé does little to forward the Adams administration's policy agenda. He's soundly defeated for reelection in 1828 by Andrew Jackson. In the end, the electorate, upon contemplating Adams's sagging credibility (and saggy backside), concludes: "The emperor has no clothes."

**after
THOUGHTS:**

Benjamin Franklin and President Teddy Roosevelt were also said to be fans of skinny-dipping. But the media never caught them with their pants down.

Why is
DUMBO WEARING HIKING BOOTS?

the
BAD
IDEA:

Insist that an elephant can't climb the Alps.

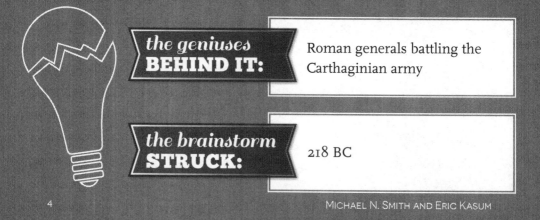

the geniuses
BEHIND IT: Roman generals battling the Carthaginian army

the brainstorm
STRUCK: 218 BC

bring on the BLUNDER:

In the brutal war between Rome and Carthage, the Carthaginians deploy what might be considered the polar opposite of a stealth weapon: big, gray, hulking, 11,000-pound elephants.

Invading Gaul (today's France) with over 50,000 troops and thirty-seven pachyderms, Hannibal's troops wreak stomping, earth-shaking terror on enemy foot soldiers while en route to the city of Rome.

from bad TO WORSE:

But the towering, treacherous Alps stand in Hannibal's path. Overconfident Roman military leaders assure their emperor that the Carthaginian forces will never, ever be able to move their elephants over the mountains. Rome, let it be known, is safe.

Yet Hannibal and his men brave blinding snow and steeply unforgiving Alpine terrain—losing half their army and almost all their elephants—to descend virtually unopposed into Italy's lush green Po Valley.

dumb LUCK:

With a hard-earned foothold in Italy, Hannibal destroys more than twenty larger, better-equipped Roman legions while sacking over four hundred towns in a sixteen-year rampage through enemy territory. The city of Rome, it's clear, is his for the taking. But he never gives the order to attack, a mystery that remains to this day.

after THOUGHTS:

A transcendent tactical genius, Hannibal and his exploits are required reading at military academies today. He's been studied by commanders from Napoleon to General George Patton to General Norman Schwarzkopf, who utilizes Hannibal's strategies of diversion in the first Gulf War.

A CONFUSED CHAUFFEUR *starts a* WORLD WAR

the BAD IDEA:

Chauffeur your country's future leader into an assassin's sights.

the genius BEHIND IT: Limo driver Leopold Lojka

the brainstorm STRUCK: June 28, 1914

MICHAEL N. SMITH AND ERIC KASUM

Ensconced in the backseat of his open-roofed Double Phaeton limousine, Archduke Franz Ferdinand, heir to the throne of the Austro-Hungarian empire, *warily* motorcades from a town hall meeting through the streets of Sarajevo, Bosnia.

And with good reason. Just hours earlier, the archduke narrowly escapes a bomb-thrower's assassination attempt. More than twenty well-wishers standing along his parade route are injured in the blast. Hoping to visit the victims and offer condolences, Ferdinand instructs his limo driver, Leopold Lojka, to brave a Serbian-anarchist-infested neighborhood and head for the local hospital. Lojka obliges but takes a wrong turn and drives down a narrow backstreet.

**from bad
TO WORSE:**

Gavrilo Princip, a Serbian Black Hand militant, can't believe his luck. Walking out of a nearby delicatessen—disappointed that his coconspirators' bomb missed its mark earlier that day—he suddenly, astonishingly, finds Ferdinand slowly passing right in front of him.

Seizing the moment, Princip pulls his gun, runs up to the undefended car, and shoots the archduke dead.

**dumb
LUCK:**

Lojka's decision to take the road less traveled delivers the archduke to his killer on a silver platter—igniting the powder keg that explodes into World War I.

**after
THOUGHTS:**

A total of sixteen coconspirators are tried and convicted of Ferdinand's murder. Princip dies of tuberculosis in prison just four years later. A total of 24 million people go on to lose their lives in the war.

The GREAT LEAP FORWARD FALLS ON ITS FACE

the BAD IDEA: Attempt to change an age-old agrarian economy—practically overnight—into a world leader in steel production by building backyard blast furnaces.

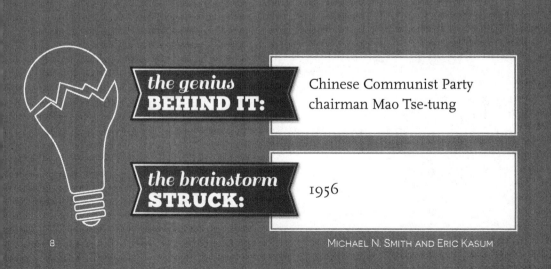

the genius BEHIND IT: Chinese Communist Party chairman Mao Tse-tung

the brainstorm STRUCK: 1956

MICHAEL N. SMITH AND ERIC KASUM

bring on the BLUNDER:

As the most recent world war has clearly demonstrated, the countries with the greatest industrial power now leverage the greatest *international* power.

Acknowledging this fact of transglobal life—while recognizing that his nation's subsistence agrarian economy leaves it poorly positioned for preeminence—Chairman Mao in 1956 decides that China needs to stop growing food plants and start opening manufacturing plants.

from bad TO WORSE:

Under his "Great Leap Forward," more than 23,000 commune-based steel plants are created. Using homemade backyard blast furnaces, kitchen utensils, old farm machinery, and anything metal that's not nailed down are *melted* down in a frantic effort to meet ambitious steel-production quotas. But the output is erratic and the quality is poor.

dumb LUCK:

Not surprisingly, with attention focused on steel, agricultural production falls precipitously. With 680 million hungry mouths to feed, famine sets in. Conservative estimates peg deaths from starvation at 20 to 25 million. By 1961, Mao reluctantly ends his disastrous experiment. Farmers-turned-steelmakers return to their now-fallow fields to begin the arduous process of salvaging their former ways of life.

after THOUGHTS:

In the Great Leap Forward's wake, dissent toward Mao's leadership grows. In response, he commences a brutal crackdown known as the Cultural Revolution, much to the dismay of human rights advocates worldwide. Ironically, China is today the largest producer and consumer of steel as well as the fastest-growing industrial power on Earth.

PAY ME NOW or I'LL SPLAY YOU LATER

the BAD IDEA: Refuse to pay the mercenaries who protect your kingdom.

the genius BEHIND IT: Vortigern, King of the Britons

the brainstorm STRUCK: Fifth century AD

bring on the BLUNDER: The wild and woolly Visigoths have just sacked Rome. Pax Romana is now looking more like grated Romano.

As the defeated Roman army retreats from the Isles of Briton (today's Great Britain), cunning local tribal chieftain Vortigern seeks to fill the void, shrewdly hiring Saxon (a.k.a. German) mercenaries to fuel his bellicose ascension to the throne. Yet once successfully seated on said throne, Vortigern pompously declares that he doesn't need to pay those pesky mercenaries—after all, he's now the omnipotent king.

from bad TO WORSE:

News flash: Bloodthirsty mercenaries really don't like not being paid. So, unsurprisingly, they turn on their former benefactor. Battle-hardened former mercenaries (and twin brothers) Hengist and Horsa lead Saxon forces to promptly lay waste to Vortigern's mercenary-less army and lay claim to a large chunk of his kingdom.

Legend has it that Hengist and Horsa then lure one hundred of Vortigern's most powerful fellow Brits to a "peace treaty" (or should we say "piece" treaty?), where each of them is cut to pieces in what becomes known as "The Night of the Long Knives." Vortigern escapes, fleeing to parts unknown.

dumb LUCK:

With Vortigern's conquered island kingdom now open and undefended, hordes of Germans brave North Sea waters to stake their claim, forever infusing Briton's language, culture, and traditions with a distinctly Anglo-Saxon character.

after THOUGHTS:

Today, thanks in no small measure to Vortigern's misstep, Brits, Americans, and much of the civilized world speak a language, derived from the Anglia region of Germany, known as English.

TIPPECANOE *and* PREZ FOR A MONTH *too*

the BAD IDEA:

Ignore the cold Washington, DC, weather and refuse to wear an overcoat to your inaugural festivities.

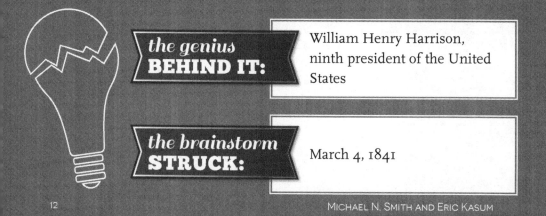

| *the genius* **BEHIND IT:** | William Henry Harrison, ninth president of the United States |

| *the brainstorm* **STRUCK:** | March 4, 1841 |

MICHAEL N. SMITH AND ERIC KASUM

bring on the BLUNDER:

When it comes to tough-as-nails military leaders, William Henry Harrison is like Rambo, General Patton, and G.I. Joe all rolled into one. Famed as a cunning Indian-fighter in leading the victorious U.S. Army in the Battle of Tippecanoe, the celebrated General Harrison—later governor of the Indiana Territory, and then a senator from Ohio before winning the presidency in 1840—is known for his canny mind, with a knack for sound tactical thinking. That is, until he makes an exceedingly *dumb* tactical decision.

from bad TO WORSE:

At the time the oldest man to be elected president, the sixty-seven-year-old Harrison decides to demonstrate his robust health by attending his inaugural festivities—held outdoors on this cold, wet March day—without wearing an overcoat or hat.

dumb LUCK:

In fact, the chilled, dripping-wet president gives the longest inaugural address in history (nearly two hours) before riding the streets of Washington in a lengthy parade. Not surprisingly, he catches a heavy cold. Within three weeks, he develops pneumonia and pleurisy. A week later, he's dead—just 31.5 days into his administration, the shortest presidential term ever.

after THOUGHTS:

When it comes to navigating that era's turbulent economic waters—with Americans still reeling from the financial panics of 1837 and 1839—Old Tippecanoe tips his canoe...and sinks it. The first U.S. chief executive to die in office, he leaves his wife penniless. Congress later votes to grant her a widow's pension (the equivalent of $500,000 today)—plus free mailing privileges for life.

FRIDAY THE 13TH:
The Original
HORROR STORY

 *the*
BAD
IDEA: Order the Knights Templar to be arrested, tortured, and burned at the stake.

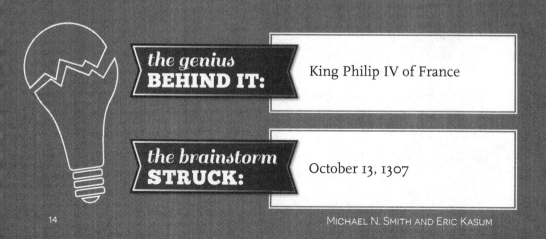

the genius
BEHIND IT: King Philip IV of France

the brainstorm
STRUCK: October 13, 1307

MICHAEL N. SMITH AND ERIC KASUM

bring on the BLUNDER:

King Philip is deeply in debt to the Knights Templar, a group of Christian crusaders who have become extraordinarily wealthy and influential during his reign.

In an effort to reclaim his regal preeminence (and wipe out his mounting debt), the king, on Friday the 13th of October, arrests the knights on suspicion of denying Christ, worshiping idols, and spitting on the crucifix. Confessions are extracted through torture. And each is sentenced to a terrible fiery death at the stake.

from bad TO WORSE:

While flames are leaping up his body, the Grand Master of the Knights Templar, Jacques de Molay, is said to have placed a curse on King Philip IV and Pope Clement V (who had collaborated in the plot against the knights).

dumb LUCK:

The curse appears to work: King Philip and Pope Clement die within a year. Both of Philip's sons also perish, relatively young, without any male heirs. By 1328, the king's bloodline has been extinguished—and his remaining fortune has been exhausted.

after THOUGHTS:

Since de Molay's seemingly successful curse, according to historian Nathaniel Lachenmeyer, author of the book 13, Friday the 13th and the number thirteen have been considered unlucky. Need proof? Just try to find the 13th floor in any older office building or hotel. The bad-luck floor is nevermore.

PREVENTING 9/11
could have been an
OPEN-AND-SHUT CASE

the BAD IDEA: Protect the privacy of a suspicious foreign operative by repeatedly refusing to open his confiscated laptop.

the geniuses BEHIND IT:

The FBI privacy police

the brainstorm STRUCK:

August 16, 2001

bring on the BLUNDER:

Acting on a tip from an apprehensive flight school instructor, FBI and INS agents lower the boom on a Moroccan French student in Minnesota, arresting him on immigration violations. In his possession, curiously, are a laptop computer, two knives, 747 flight manuals, and crop dusting information.

One of the arresting FBI agents, Harry Samit, asks his superiors for permission to investigate the contents of the confiscated laptop. Their response, citing privacy issues: "Request denied."

Concerned that the suspect might have nefarious intentions, the FBI's Minnesota bureau sends dozens of communiqués to FBI brass asking for access to the computer. Requests denied.

Agent Colleen Rowley makes an appeal to search the suspect's apartment. Request denied. Frustrated, Samit pleads with FBI headquarters to pass information about the laptop to the Secret Service for further investigation. Request (you guessed it) denied again.

**from bad
TO WORSE:**

Tragically, just three weeks after the suspect's arrest, the World Trade Center towers collapse under a modern-day Kamikaze attack. Nearly 3,000 people are killed in a trio of terrorist strikes in New York, Washington, DC, and Pennsylvania.

Only after these attacks do FBI leaders allow the controversial laptop to be analyzed. On it is a nightmare come true: the names and phone numbers of the entire al-Qaeda terrorist chain of command, details of the September 11 plot on the World Trade Center, plus the names of several of the nineteen hijackers.

**dumb
LUCK:**

The laptop, you see, belongs to Zacarias Moussaoui, who, if not arrested, would have been the 20th hijacker. And had his computer been analyzed sooner, the entire 9/11 disaster might have been averted.

**after
THOUGHTS:**

In the wake of his role in the worst terrorist attack ever on U.S. soil, Moussaoui is sentenced to life in prison in Colorado. In October 2001, the Patriot Act is passed, allowing law-enforcement authorities clearer access to the personal information of suspected foreign operatives.

The A‑‑‑‑IN's GUNSHOT *that* BACKFIRES BIG TIME

the
BAD IDEA:

Attempt to tear apart the fragile Union by assassinating key political leaders.

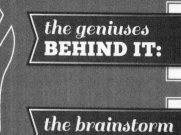

the geniuses
BEHIND IT: John Wilkes Booth and his coconspirators

the brainstorm
STRUCK: 1865

MICHAEL N. SMITH AND ERIC KASUM

You might say that John Wilkes Booth, the hunky stage actor critically acclaimed as "the handsomest man in America," is the Brad Pitt of his day.

Yet below his chiseled cheekbones, a dark rage lurks. A Confederate sympathizer vehemently opposed to Northern hegemony, Booth vows vengeance against President Abraham Lincoln for the Emancipation Proclamation and the South's defeat in the Civil War.

from bad
TO WORSE:

Conspiring with eight like-minded men, he conjures up a daring plan to simultaneously assassinate Lincoln, Vice President Andrew Johnson, and Secretary of State William Seward. On April 14, 1865, while Lincoln enjoys a performance of the popular play *Our American Cousin* from his box in Washington's Ford's Theatre, the famous thespian sneaks up from behind and fires a bullet into the president's head. The next morning, Lincoln is dead.

dumb
LUCK:

Yet Booth's single shot becomes perhaps the biggest backfire in American history. Hoping his murderous act would aggrandize him as a conquering hero, Booth instead becomes the focus of national outrage. Within twelve days, he's hunted down by the Union army—and killed.

Over 30 million people line the route of the president's funeral train in tribute to their fallen leader's ideals—and in permanent repudiation of Booth's dream of a separate South.

after
THOUGHTS:

On the night Lincoln is shot, Seward survives an attack by a knife-wielding Booth henchman. And Johnson's "killer" chickens out.

Sure, HE WAS A MURDERING MARAUDER, but At Least WE GET A DAY OFF

 the **BAD IDEA:**

Columbus Day.

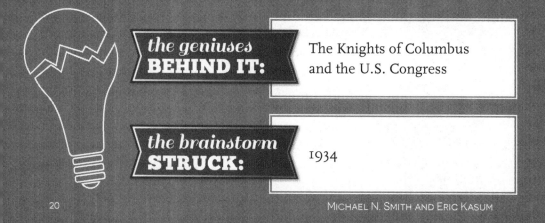

the geniuses BEHIND IT: The Knights of Columbus and the U.S. Congress

the brainstorm STRUCK: 1934

bring on the BLUNDER:

Alleged fact: Christopher Columbus is the discoverer of America. *Actual fact:* Eric the Red discovers it five hundred years prior. And let's not forget the Native Americans who happened upon our continent thousands of years before the Europeans arrived.

Alleged fact: Columbus benevolently engages the indigenous people he encounters. *Actual fact:* According to detailed journals kept by his crewmen and extensive diaries written by local missionaries, Columbus and his men work the natives to the point of death. Young girls are sold into sex slavery. On one day, a Catholic priest claims to witness Columbus's crew—with good old Chris's knowledge—rape and/or dismember thousands of local men, women, and children.

from bad TO WORSE:

Within sixty-five years of the intrepid adventurer setting foot on American soil, over one million natives have been killed. Still more have been sold into slavery.

dumb LUCK:

Despite all this, Congress—under pressure from the Knights of Columbus and as a sop to the growing Italian immigrant population in the United States—in 1934 establishes the first national holiday honoring, in essence, a criminal: Columbus Day.

after THOUGHTS:

Why does history continue to ignore these dastardly deeds and lionize Columbus? The answer is unclear. But maybe, as M. N. Pokrovsky once wrote: "History is nothing more than the politics of today projected into the events of the past."

By George, That
LIBRARY BOOK *is*
80,665 DAYS LATE

the
BAD
IDEA: Lend a book to President George Washington.

**the geniuses
BEHIND IT:**

The New York Society Library

**the brainstorm
STRUCK:**

1789

**bring on the
BLUNDER:**

He's busy forging a dynamic new nation. He's busy defining the American presidency. He's busy commander-in-chiefing the U.S. Army. He's even busy meticulously remodeling his spacious Mount Vernon estate.

So is it any wonder George Washington is too busy to do something as mundane as return a book he borrowed from the local library?

from bad TO WORSE:

His hectic schedule aside, Washington, five months into the first term of his presidency, checks out a highbrow tome titled *The Law of Nations* and volume 12 of *The Commons Debates* from the New York Society Library (in what was then the nation's capital) on October 5, 1789.

One month later, the books are overdue. A few years later, the library's lending records go missing. And on December 14, 1799, Washington dies—having forgotten to return the literature he borrowed ten years earlier.

dumb LUCK:

Fast-forward two centuries. Matthew Haugen, archivist of the library, in 2010 stumbles upon dusty records that show Washington never returned the books. Turns out the father of our country has rung up the mother of all library fines: Adjusted for inflation over 221 years, it amounts to a whopping $300,000—quite possibly the largest penalty of its kind in history.

after THOUGHTS:

Notified of their patriarch's malfeasance, staffers at Washington's Mount Vernon estate, unable to locate either of the books, scour the world and locate an identical edition of *The Law of Nations*. The $12,000 book is purchased and handed over to the library, which immediately forgives Washington's rather sizable fine.

BONES *of* CONTENTION PILT ON A LIE

the BAD IDEA:

Piltdown Man.

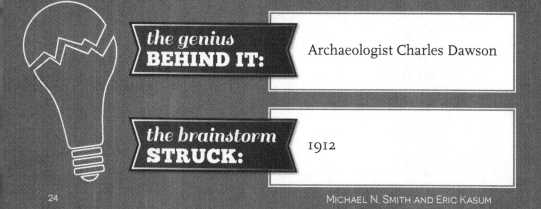

the genius **BEHIND IT:**	Archaeologist Charles Dawson

| *the brainstorm* **STRUCK:** | 1912 |

MICHAEL N. SMITH AND ERIC KASUM

Based on the discovery of Neanderthal Man (1856, in Germany), Cro-Magnon Man (1868, in France), and Heidelberg Man (1907, also in Germany), human-kind's first steps seem to have been taken on the mainland of Europe.

In response, British archaeologists work feverishly to outdo their French and German rivals in an effort to uncover the "missing link" on English soil. Britain, they believe, must rightfully lay claim to what Darwin terms "the origins of man."

**from bad
TO WORSE:**

Propitiously, in 1912, amateur archaeologist Charles Dawson stumbles upon Piltdown Man—ancient skull fragments uncovered in an English quarry that appear to be part man, part ape. Yet suspicions arise. How did the missing jaw suddenly appear at the site four years into the dig? Soon, the Royal College challenges Dawson's findings.

**dumb
LUCK:**

By the 1950s, as the discovery of *Australopithecus africanus* points to Africa as home to the earliest humans, scientists come to consider Piltdown a strange, disconnected evolutionary side road. Then, in 1953, *Time* magazine publishes evidence that the Piltdown Man fossil is actually constructed of a medieval human skull and the jaw of a five-hundred-year-old orangutan, each stained with chemicals to appear older. Piltdown, it's revealed, has been a hoax. Dawson, now deceased, had been a fraud.

**after
THOUGHTS:**

British scientists, in their nationalistic zeal, had been too accepting of Dawson's shaky assertions. As a result, Piltdown Man leads the world's archaeologists down a blind alley that sets evolutionary science back decades.

IF YOU'RE ANTI-NUKE, THIS WILL REALLY HIT YOUR HOT BUTTON

the BAD IDEA:

"The Button."

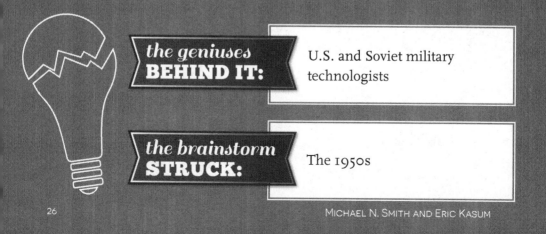

the geniuses **BEHIND IT:**	U.S. and Soviet military technologists
the brainstorm **STRUCK:**	The 1950s

MICHAEL N. SMITH AND ERIC KASUM

bring on the BLUNDER:

No, it's not the one you hit to change the TV channel. Or the one on your waistband that bursts across the room when you've gobble-gobbled too much Thanksgiving dinner. Rather, it's that special one that can start World War III.

Yes, friends, we're talking about "The Button." It's the handy-dandy device that gives Cold War American presidents and Soviet premiers the power to launch a nuclear strike with the press of a pinkie. And it's nearly ended humanity far too many times in the past half century.

from bad TO WORSE:

Example: The Cuban Missile Crisis, October 1962. The U.S. places one hundred nuclear missiles in Europe, close enough to strike Moscow. The USSR responds by secretly sending the same to Cuba, mere minutes by missile from Washington, DC. President John F. Kennedy's military advisors urge him to push the button, thereby launching a preemptive strike against the Cuban missile installations.

dumb LUCK:

Instead, Kennedy waits, Soviet leader Nikita Khrushchev flinches, and neither man's itchy finger touches the button. Yet the end of humanity remains at the fingertips of such political leaders across the world to this day.

after THOUGHTS:

In the years that follow, failed computer chips, flights of geese, software problems, and misidentified weather balloons prompt nuclear launch decision-makers to reach for the button. As of this writing, Armageddon (other than in the form of a bad Michael Bay movie) has not yet arrived.

The MIDNIGHT WALK *of* PAUL REVERE

the BAD IDEA:

Credit the wrong man with alerting American colonists to an imminent British invasion.

the genius BEHIND IT: Poet Henry Wadsworth Longfellow

the brainstorm STRUCK: 1860

MICHAEL N. SMITH AND ERIC KASUM

bring on the BLUNDER:

Every schoolkid knows Longfellow's classic poem that begins: "Listen my children and you shall hear of the midnight ride of Paul Revere..."

But hold your horses! Historians tell us that Longfellow ignored as many as forty other brave riders, including a young man who rode farther and alerted more Massachusetts colonists to the impending British raid than Paul Revere *ever* did.

from bad TO WORSE:

Here's how the real story unfolds: Just hours after Paul Revere makes his legendary 20-mile ride, he's captured by a British patrol. His horse confiscated, Revere walks into Lexington escorted by an armed guard.

Meanwhile, twenty-three-year-old Israel Bissell gallops off for Worcester, shouting: "To arms! To arms! The war has begun!" Amazingly, he completes the daylong ride in two hours, collapsing his exhausted horse under him. On a fresh mount, he then tirelessly races from Massachusetts to Philadelphia—covering a full 350 miles in just six days.

dumb LUCK:

Despite his relatively puny accomplishment, the "revered" Revere today symbolizes the courageous spirit of the American Revolution. Meanwhile, Bissell is a name better known for, well, vacuum cleaners.

after THOUGHTS:

In 1995, a poet finally gave Bissell his just recognition, penning the words: "Listen my children to my epistle/Of the long, long ride of Israel Bissell." Just doesn't have the same ring to it, eh?

CAPTURED SLAVE SHIP *sets the* ABOLITIONIST MOVEMENT FREE

the BAD IDEA:

Imprison Africans bound for slavery in America.

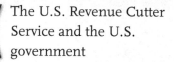

The wildly lucrative yet starkly inhumane transatlantic slave trade—outlawed since 1808—continues for decades, even as the U.S. Revenue Cutter Service, charged with reducing seaborne smuggling and enforcing tariffs, ratchets up enforcement.

**from bad
TO WORSE:**

Fast-forward to 1839. Joseph Cinque leads a group of fifty-four Africans aboard the Spanish slave schooner *La Amistad* in a daring mutiny near Havana, Cuba, demanding that the crew provide them safe passage home.

Instead, *Amistad*'s double-crossing navigator sails the unsuspecting would-be slaves north to Long Island, where the Revenue Cutter Service immediately impounds the ship and its human cargo, claiming a portion of its monetary value for the U.S. government, as the law allows.

**dumb
LUCK:**

President Martin Van Buren's administration, weary of tariff-evading smugglers and sympathetic to the proslavery views of wealthy landowners, argues for the government's financial share of *Amistad*'s slave payload—all the way to the Supreme Court. There, former president John Quincy Adams cites the freedoms outlined in the Declaration of Independence in passionately counterclaiming that the Africans have been illegally imprisoned by the feds. In 1841, the high court agrees, ruling that the thirty-five surviving participants in the *Amistad* uprising are free to return to Africa.

**after
THOUGHTS:**

In an ill-fated effort to ignore the burgeoning abolitionist movement in America, the Van Buren administration actually helped stoke the antislavery fires that later erupt into the Civil War.

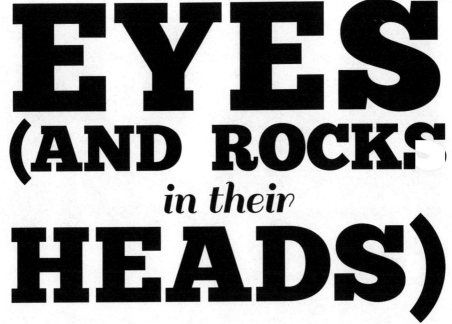

ENTERTAINERS WITH STARS in their EYES (AND ROCKS in their HEADS)

How to LIP-SINK *a* MUSIC CAREER

the BAD IDEA:

Create a pop music group led by two singers who can't sing.

the genius **BEHIND IT:**	Frank Farian, übersuccessful German music producer
the brainstorm **STRUCK:**	1988

Farian is looking for the "next big thing" in music. Scouring the '80s Berlin club scene, he happens upon models Fabrice Morvan and Rob Pilatus tearing up the dance floor. To most, they're no more than hunky, prancing boy toys. But to Farian, they're ideal front men for a new band. Soon, the pop group Milli Vanilli is born.

One problem: Neither Rob nor Fab can sing. To cover that rather glaring deficiency, Farian secretly hires professional vocalists to record all Milli Vanilli songs—and directs Rob and Fab to lip-synch to these recordings whenever performing live.

from bad
TO WORSE:

Milli Vanilli takes off like a hip-hopping missile. Then, just as quickly, the missile explodes. At a 1989 MTV live concert, Rob and Fab are lip-synching and gyrating to their monster hit "Girl You Know It's True" when the recording skips—forcing them to repeat the same line of the song over and over. The Milli Vanilli fraud is exposed!

dumb
LUCK:

Outraged fans demand that the musical impostors be strung up by their dreadlocks. Dozens of lawsuits follow. Arista Records breaks their recording contract. The band's Best New Artist Grammy Award is returned in shame. Their short-lived careers in disarray, Fab slips into obscurity and Rob dies of a drug overdose in 1998.

after
THOUGHTS:

In the wake of the Milli Vanilli debacle, lip-synching has become a hot topic among music critics and fans today, with everyone from Britney to Bieber to Beyoncé being accused of "fake singing" a live performance.

E.T.'S MISSION *to* MARS ABORTED

the BAD IDEA: Turn down perhaps the greatest product placement opportunity in movie history.

the geniuses BEHIND IT:

The chocolate-covered nuts at Mars, Inc.

the brainstorm STRUCK:

June 11, 1981

bring on the BLUNDER:

You know the movie. You know the scene: Young Elliot lures E.T., the extraterrestrial, out of hiding with a trail of yummy candies.

According to *E.T.* screenwriter Melissa Mathison, only one candy could pique the sweet tooth of a cute, cuddly intergalactic visitor to our planet: the most popular candy on Earth—M&M's. But when presented with this pioneering product placement opportunity, the space cadets at Mars, Inc. allow the idea to fizzle on the launch pad. "We don't want an alien eating our candy," they opine. "It might frighten kids."

from bad TO WORSE:

Dauntless *E.T.* producer Kathleen Kennedy, scrambling to find an M&M's replacement, stumbles upon an obscure candy Hershey has been struggling to get off the ground for some time: Reese's Pieces. And in a deal that's truly out of this world, Hershey agrees to pay absolutely nothing for placing Reese's Pieces in the much-anticipated film—and to cross-promote the movie in their advertising at a cost of just $1 million.

As *E.T.* rockets past *Star Wars* to become the highest-grossing film of its time, Reese's Pieces sales blast off. Hershey's Jack Dowd calls the placement "the biggest marketing coup in history. We got the kind of recognition we would normally have to pay fifteen or twenty million bucks for."

dumb LUCK:

Mars, embarrassed by the *E.T.* blunder, vows never to miss another high-flying placement opportunity. U.S. space shuttle astronauts eat M&M's on subsequent missions. And on Spaceship One, the first privately financed manned space project, M&M's float colorfully around the weightless cabin.

after THOUGHTS:

With the legendary success of Reese's Pieces, the product placement industry soon enters hyperspace. Today, it continues to grow at a rate in excess of traditional print and broadcast advertising, rising over 145 percent between 2006 and 2011 alone.

G-MEN GO SCREWY SCREWY OVER "LOUIE LOUIE"

the BAD IDEA: Attempt to identify the "obscene" lyrics hidden in the hit song "Louie Louie."

the geniuses BEHIND IT: Attorney General Robert Kennedy and FBI Director J. Edgar Hoover

the brainstorm STRUCK: 1963

bring on the BLUNDER: For months, irate parents, religious groups, and moral leaders have demanded government action. No, they're not railing against the nation's escalating incursion into Vietnam. Or its inertia on the issue of civil rights. They've got more important matters on their minds—such as having the feds find out once and for all if the hit song "Louie Louie" is encouraging our young people to do the "naughty, naughty."

Written in the 1950s as a wistful, Caribbean-influenced tune about a man yearning for his girl, "Louie Louie" as originally penned in pigeon English by Richard Berry goes:

Louie Louie, oh oh, me gotta go.
Louie Louie, oh oh, me gotta go.

Fine little girl, she waits for me.
Me catch the ship, for cross the sea.

The quirky tune, unintelligibly covered in 1963 after a raucous night of partying by Oregon's the Kingsmen, soon rockets up the Top 40 charts. But, ah, rumors emerge that the lyrics contain secret smutty references to teen scx. In fact, a commonly accepted translation, allegedly audible at slower playback speed, reads:

Louie, Louie—Oh no! Grab her way down low.
Louie, Louie—Oh baby! Grab her way down low.

A fine little bitch, she waits for me,
She gets her kicks on top of me.

Word of a government obscenity investigation surges sales of the record—produced for a mere $36—into the hundreds of thousands. Yet, after a two-and-a-half-year inquiry, the FBI drops the case. Thousands of forensic man-hours spent attempting to unravel the mysteries of "Louie Louie" have led the G-men to the conclusion that the Kingsmen's lyrics couldn't possibly be obscene, because they are "unintelligible at any speed."

An enduring party classic, the "scandalous, unholy" "Louie Louie" never reaches number-one status. It's kept from the top spot, ironically, by the Singing Nun and her foreign language hit, "Dominique."

REMEMBER
THE DORKS, LUKE

the BAD IDEA: Decline to produce the film that will launch one of the most successful movie franchises in history.

the geniuses BEHIND IT: Chieftains of virtually every movie studio in Hollywood

the brainstorm STRUCK: 1976

bring on the BLUNDER: In the sparkling-water-swilling, $3,000-suit-wearing, have-your-masseuse-call-my-masseuse world of Hollywood film production, saying yes to a film concept is fraught with peril. If the movie bombs, you could lose your job (not to mention your masseuse).

So it should come as no surprise that just about every movie studio worth its back lot has a word for George Lucas when he comes calling with his trifling little fantasy film tentatively called *Star Wars*—and that word is a big, fat, Jabba-sized "No!"

from bad TO WORSE:

Unfazed (or is it "un-*phasered*?"), Lucas perseveres. Broke and in need of work after Universal Studios initially refuses to release his *American Graffiti* (made for under $1 million, it goes on to gross over $118 million), Lucas first approaches United Artists with his "space adventure" idea. They turn him down. Universal follows suit. Then others hop onto the no-way-Georgy bandwagon.

dumb LUCK:

Desperate, Lucas screens *American Graffiti* for Alan Ladd Jr., head of 20th Century Fox. He loves the movie—and inquires about any other ideas Lucas might have for future films.

Lucas introduces him to Luke, Leia, Han, Chewy, R2-D2, and the host of *Star Wars* characters now part of cinematic lore. Ladd eventually agrees to produce the movie, which ultimately earns $800 million in box office sales alone. *Star Wars* also snares seven Academy Awards in 1977, while setting the standard for the "summer blockbuster." Much, of course, to the chagrin of all those studio naysayers.

after THOUGHTS:

Other top-grossing movies (along with their earnings) initially turned down by the major studios:
Avatar (2009): $2.7 billion
Titanic (1997): $1.8 billion
Lord of the Rings (trilogy, 2001–2003): $3.3 billion
Spider-Man (trilogy, 2002–2007): $2.5 billion
Back to the Future (trilogy, 1985–1989): $1.1 billion
E.T.: The Extra-Terrestrial (1982): $792 million

DON'T TASE ME, BRO– (AND DON'T SING TO ME EITHER)

the BAD IDEA: Feature crime fighters with guns in their hands and a song in their hearts to create the musical TV drama *Cop Rock*.

the genius BEHIND IT: TV megaproducer Steven Bochco

the brainstorm STRUCK: 1990

Imagine you're sitting in front of the TV, ready for the new season's toughest, grittiest, urban police drama.

Sirens blare, tires squeal, the street thugs are on the run from our men in blue. Just as the cops are about to cuff the wrongdoers, something peculiar happens: The gang of hoodlums breaks into song. The officers counter with their own impromptu musical number. And a chorus of citizen on-lookers grooves to the beat before the hoods are hauled off to the hoosegow.

Prepare to wretch. You've just witnessed the wonder—and the blunder—of *Cop Rock*.

from bad
TO WORSE:

Banking on Bochco's success with iconic TV shows such as *Hill Street Blues*, NBC executives put aside their reservations about the celebrated producer's odd musical-crime-drama concept and order thirteen *Cop Rock* episodes for the 1990 primetime schedule.

dumb
LUCK:

On September 26, the show premieres—and its praises go unsung. Critics deem the musical drama a cringe-worthy unintentional comedy. Ratings plummet. And NBC places the show under arrest after only eleven episodes. *TV Guide*, though, does give *Cop Rock* a top-ten ranking...on its list of the fifty worst TV shows of all time.

after
THOUGHTS:

Bochco recovers, eventually winning ten Emmy Awards (none for *Cop Rock*) in creating critical and commercial hits *L.A. Law* and *NYPD Blue*. *Cop Rock* is the last musical series to hit the airwaves until more recent entries, such as *Glee* (2009), *Nashville* (2012), and *Smash* (2012).

BRITNEY BARES *all*

the BAD IDEA:

Allow your whacked-out personal life to nearly smack down a hugely successful music career.

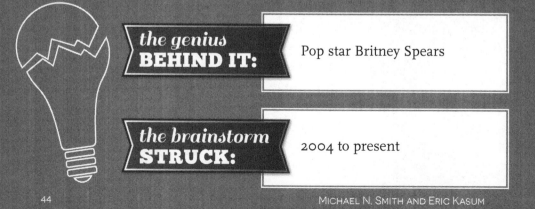

the genius BEHIND IT: Pop star Britney Spears

the brainstorm STRUCK: 2004 to present

MICHAEL N. SMITH AND ERIC KASUM

bring on the BLUNDER:

Springboarding to fame on the Disney Channel's *The All New Mickey Mouse Club* at age eight, Spears explodes into America's biggest-ever teen pop music sensation with the 25-million-selling "Baby One More Time" in 1999. But just as Spears's cumulative album sales top 52 million by 2002, she stumbles through a series of bizarre escapades that have her music-buying public pleading "Baby One *Less* Time."

from bad TO WORSE:

Exhibit A: In 2004, Spears opts to marry childhood friend Jason Allen Alexander—for a total of fifty-five hours—before being granted a writ of annulment, which embarrassingly cites Spears's "lack of understanding of her actions."

Exhibit B: Later that same year, Spears decides to marry dancer/rapper Kevin Federline following a brief three-month courtship. After a tumultuous, two-year, tabloid-covered union, the couple file for divorce.

dumb LUCK:

In 2007, after being photographed driving a luxury car with one of her young children unrestrained on her lap, Spears checks into a drug rehab facility—and checks out twenty-four hours later. The following night, she's photographed shaving her head bald at a Tarzana, California, hair salon. In rapid succession, she then loses custody of her children, is remanded to a psych ward, and is famously photographed getting out of a car open-legged and bare-crotched.

after THOUGHTS:

Spears watches her music sales drop to 3.5 million for *Circus* in 2008. Despite all of her ups and downs—or maybe because of them—her album *Femme Fatale* opens at number one on the Billboard 200 ranking in 2011.

Look, Dear, CHARLIE CHAPLIN DROPPED BY for a SLEEPOVER

the BAD IDEA:

Break into a strange home and take a nap on a kid's bed.

the genius BEHIND IT:	Actor Robert Downey Jr.
the brainstorm STRUCK:	May 1996

MICHAEL N. SMITH AND ERIC KASUM

Nominated for an Oscar in 1992 and dubbed the greatest actor of his generation, Downey, feeling "less than zero" under the influence of heroin and cocaine, speeds down Sunset Boulevard naked while packing a .357 magnum. He's soon arrested—all the while claiming to officers that his car is filled with rats—and eventually sentenced to drug rehabilitation plus probation.

from bad
TO WORSE:

While on probation, Downey, wearing nothing more than a pair of briefs and a smile, stumbles drunkenly into an unoccupied Malibu home and falls asleep on a child's bed. When the homeowners return to find the *Chaplin* star cutting Zs in their kid's room, he's again arrested—and again sentenced to rehab and probation.

Upon missing a court-ordered drug test a short time later, he's sentenced to four months in LA County jail. After his release, with his once-promising career on the wane, he skips another drug test and is sentenced to three years in state prison. Producers of TV's *Ally McBeal* end his recurring role.

dumb
LUCK:

In 2003, Downey's free fall from the heights of Hollywood hits rock bottom. Unemployable, he summons the courage to toss his drugs into the blue Pacific and enter a phase of intensive rehabilitation. He claims to have been clean and sober ever since.

after
THOUGHTS:

Completing his comeback, Downey is nominated as best supporting actor for his race-bending role in the 2008 comedy *Tropic Thunder* and goes on to soar as Iron Man in the hit film trilogy.

SMOKEY,
Not Stirred

the BAD IDEA: Turn down the iconic role of 007 in the wildly popular James Bond film series.

the genius BEHIND IT:

Burt Reynolds

the brainstorm STRUCK:

1972

bring on the BLUNDER:

Fresh from his star turn as the macho river adventurer Lewis in 1972's best picture Oscar-nominee *Deliverance*—plus his buzz-inducing, seminude spread in *Cosmopolitan* magazine—Burt Reynolds is the hottest actor in Hollywood. First in line for the most coveted parts, Reynolds is presented with the mother of all leading man roles: James Bond.

In a mad scramble to secure a dashing actor "who can wear the tux, tote the pistol, and woo the girl," megaproducer Albert Broccoli has Reynolds squarely in his sights.

Proclaiming "[a] American can't play James Bond," Reynolds instead opts to make such cinematic stinkers as *Fuzz*, *White Lightning*, and *The Man Who Loved Cat Dancing* over the next two years.

The jilted Broccoli settles for the tongue-in-cheek savoir faire of Roger Moore to carry the Bond tradition forward, a billion-dollar bonanza that lasts twelve full years. In that time, Reynolds flexes his star power to make such forgettable flops as *Gator*, *WW and the Dixie Dance Kings*, and two *Smokey and the Bandit* gems.

His leading man élan squandered, the now-aging sex symbol falls out of favor with Hollywood in the 1980s. Having foregone the potentially huge Bond-movie paydays, he files for bankruptcy in 1996.

Lampooning the actor's questionable career choices, comedian Robert Wuhl once joked: "Burt Reynolds makes so many bad movies that when someone *else* makes a bad movie, Burt gets a royalty." In a 2005 interview, a regretful Reynolds admits, "Now, in the middle of the night, you hear me wake up in this cold sweat saying, 'Bond, James Bond.'"

C.APONE'S TREASURE
Turns into TRASH TV

the BAD IDEA: "The Mystery of Al Capone's Vault."

---

the geniuses BEHIND IT:

Tribune Entertainment and WGN, Chicago

the brainstorm STRUCK:

April 1986

bring on the BLUNDER:

A slick-talking tough guy from the streets of New York and his network of henchmen plot to bust open a safe and walk off with a big payday. But when it comes time to deliver the goods, they welsh.

Sounds like the kind of misguided caper that in the age of the mafia mobster might have gotten the perpetrators whacked. But in the end, it's 30 million unsuspecting Americans (and the slick New Yorker's career) that take the hit.

from bad TO WORSE:

Recently fired as a muckraking investigative reporter for ABC News, Geraldo Rivera agrees to host a two-hour live TV event—an event that promises to reveal the contents of a secret vault located in the basement of Chicago's abandoned Lexington Hotel, onetime headquarters of the 1920s organized crime syndicate run by the notorious Al Capone.

The show begins with a breathless Rivera hurrying live TV viewers into the ghostly, spider-webbed hotel basement. He points out Capone's labyrinth of tunnels (For hiding treasure? For dumping dead bodies?) winding through the bowels of the building. He then teases the show's climactic revelation: the breaching of a twenty-two-inch concrete wall, behind which could lie the Capone gang's vaulted riches.

dumb LUCK:

With over 30 million people watching on over 181 stations around the world, the excavation team, deep into the long-winded show, at last breaks through the massive wall.

TV lights scour the darkened inner chamber for signs of lost treasure or grizzly body parts. Instead, the audience sees nothing but random trash, dirt piles, and empty booze bottles. The program ends, as Capone might have said, with one big, fat "fuhgeddaboudit."

after THOUGHTS:

Despite attracting, at the time, the biggest syndicated audience in TV history, the show turns Geraldo and his producers into laughingstocks across the nation. Writing in his 1991 autobiography, Rivera admits that he has helped make "Al Capone's vault" a modern euphemism for any overhyped event doomed to disappointing results.

DINOSAUR HELPS BRING ACTOR'S FINANCES *to the* BRINK *of* EXTINCTION

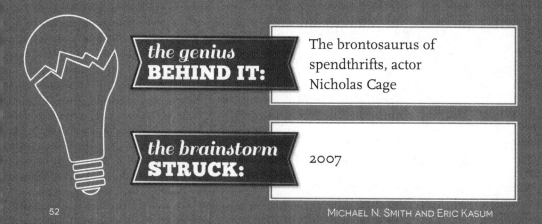

the BAD IDEA:

Spend over a quarter of a million dollars on dinosaur remains instead of paying your income taxes.

the genius BEHIND IT:

The brontosaurus of spendthrifts, actor Nicholas Cage

the brainstorm STRUCK:

2007

MICHAEL N. SMITH AND ERIC KASUM

 bring on the BLUNDER:

He's bought a jet. Two yachts. Three castles. Two Bahamian islands. A gaggle of mansions. Fifty cars (including a $495,000 Lamborghini). And a comic book collection worth $1.6 million.

But what he really needs—above all other worldly possessions—is a 67-million-year-old dinosaur skull. So *Raising Arizona* star Nicholas Cage raises the auction ante and outbids fellow thespian Leonardo DiCaprio to snare the prehistoric relic for $276,000.

from bad TO WORSE:

Boneheaded move, right? But here's where the dino dung hits the fan: Cage already owes the government over $6 million in back taxes. And his bizarre public pirouette into paleontology has helped incur the wrath of the IRS.

As the tax man closes in on Cage, the actor reverses course, turning his years-long buying spree into a bargain basement sell-off, listing his Bel-Air mansion for millions of dollars less than its original asking price—then losing hundreds of thousands on the sale of his castles (including one in which he spent just one night). Even his beloved vintage Superman comics need to go.

dumb LUCK:

Aiming to focus more attention on his finances (he earns millions a year), Cage hires a new business manager in 2008. And with a nod to his alcohol-addled, Oscar-nominated role in *Leaving Las Vegas*, he reportedly pledges to take a more sober approach to spending.

 after THOUGHTS:

Adding to his reputation for eccentricity, Cage claims he's been stalked by a mysterious mime since making *Bringing Out the Dead* in 1999.

PETE DOES HIS BEST TO AVOID THE LONG AND WINDING ROAD *to* SUPERSTARDOM

the BAD IDEA: Refuse to dress like, talk to, or generally fit in with your soon-to-be hugely popular bandmates.

the genius BEHIND IT:

Pete Best, drummer for the Quarrymen

the brainstorm STRUCK:

1960

bring on the BLUNDER:

Years before the "do-your-own-thing" hippie zeitgeist comes into vogue, Pete Best is already traveling to the beat of a different drum.

His bandmates wear leather jackets and coif their hair in a mop-top style. Pete wears short sleeves and sticks with his naturally curly locks. His bandmates hang out together. Pete quietly saunters off alone. So in light of his steadfast refusal to get with the program, Best is sacked as drummer for the Quarrymen, a small, little-known Liverpool pop/rock group that has now assumed a catchy new name: the Beatles.

MICHAEL N. SMITH AND ERIC KASUM

Some speculate that core members John Lennon, Paul McCartney, and George Harrison vote to fire Best in favor of the quirky, homely Ringo Starr not because of Pete's stubborn independence but rather for something far more personal: jealousy. After all, Best is widely considered the most handsome of the early Beatles, wildly cheered and hotly pursued by the band's female fans.

Hurt and bewildered by the firing, Best turns down an offer from Beatles manager Brian Epstein to build him a new band. Instead, he sits home and sulks, reluctant to venture outside and face the music about his dismissal.

dumb
LUCK:

As Beatle hit after hit after hit skyrockets up the charts, Best is signed to Decca Records—and releases a single that flops. He forms a new band, the Pete Best Combo, which tours with little success. In desperation, Pete records an album not-so-cleverly titled *Best of the Beatles*, a ham-handed play on the drummer's last name and former band. Believing the album to be a Beatles greatest hits compilation, angry record buyers are not amused.

after
THOUGHTS:

As Beatlemania reaches uncharted heights worldwide, a despondent Best contemplates suicide. Quitting music, he takes a low-level job delivering bread. Ironically, the man who's lost his job as a member of what is now the most successful entertainment act of all time then becomes the manager of a job training and placement center in Liverpool. He remains outside the music business for two decades.

RAIDERS *of* *the* LOST PART

the BAD IDEA:

Turn down the now-legendary movie role of Indiana Jones.

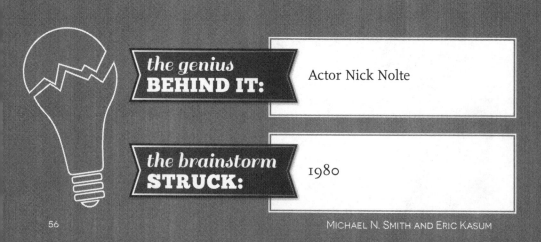

the genius BEHIND IT:	Actor Nick Nolte

the brainstorm STRUCK:	1980

MICHAEL N. SMITH AND ERIC KASUM

bring on the BLUNDER:

Refusing to don the fedora and crack the bullwhip, Nolte declines the choice role of Indiana Jones in George Lucas's modern classic *Raiders of the Lost Ark*—with a hearty thank-you from Harrison Ford.

from bad TO WORSE:

Instead of assuming the mantle of the two-fisted, Nazi-fighting professor, Nolte decides instead to star in the long-since-forgotten *Heart Beat*.

Ironically, just three years earlier, Nolte had already lost the iconic role of Han Solo in Lucas's *Star Wars: A New Hope* to the aforementioned Ford. That's the same Harrison Ford who goes on to make a total of four highly successful *Indiana Jones* films over the next three decades.

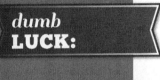

dumb LUCK:

All told, the quartet of Indy movies earn over $1.9 billion worldwide—and help make Ford one of the three most successful actors in box-office history.

after THOUGHTS:

Nolte is also director Richard Donner's first choice to play the man of steel in the 1978 feature hit *Superman*. But alas, he's bypassed (under pressure from the studios to cast a beefier, more handsome actor) in favor of relatively unknown Christopher Reeve—who quickly catapults to fame and fortune faster than a speeding bullet.

Ted Danson's
MINSTREL CRAMP

the BAD IDEA: Perform a profane comedy routine—in blackface.

the genius BEHIND IT: Actor/liberal activist Ted Danson

the brainstorm STRUCK: October 1993

bring on the BLUNDER: With the nation still reeling—and Los Angeles still smoldering—from the March 1991 police beating of African American man Rodney King, followed by the April 1992 LA riots in minority communities, race is a red-hot issue in early 1990s America.

Yet former *Cheers* jokester Ted Danson decides to fete his then-girlfriend Whoopi Goldberg at a Friars Club Roast with an N-word-laden monologue staged in the disgraced, discredited, and decidedly racist greasepaint makeup known as blackface.

MICHAEL N. SMITH AND ERIC KASUM

from bad TO WORSE:

Despite a Friars Club tradition of anything-goes, X-rated, sexually/ethnically/racially repugnant roast humor, Danson's routine is excoriated by the media, advocacy groups, and the general public—each charging that it's blatantly bigoted.

Danson is inundated with threats and hate mail. The head of the Friars Club publicly apologizes for Danson's performance. New York City mayor David Dinkins and other African American leaders offer condemnation. Goldberg, an Oscar-winning African American actress, reacts by defending her man, claiming to have written some of the most incendiary jokes herself—and admitting to having hired the makeup artist who painted his face.

dumb LUCK:

In a torrent of public outcry, the couple calls it quits shortly after the minstrel mishap. Danson's relationship with Goldberg, which has already resulted in a whopping $25-million divorce settlement with his second wife, has now also wounded his public image as a racially sensitive, Hollywood liberal activist.

after THOUGHTS:

Danson, responding to media inquiries about his off-color comedy routine, skirts the issue by stating: "I understand your curiosity, but I've finally matured enough to have a private life, and I shall guard it jealously." After a string of moderately successful movies in the late 1990s, Danson returns to TV in 1998 with a triumphant seven-year run in the CBS series *Becker*—and in 2011 as a regular on the hit crime drama *CSI*.

Snuff Daddy's GREATEST HIT

the BAD IDEA: Snort your dead father's ashes.

the genius BEHIND IT: Rolling Stones guitarist Keith Richards

the brainstorm STRUCK: 2002

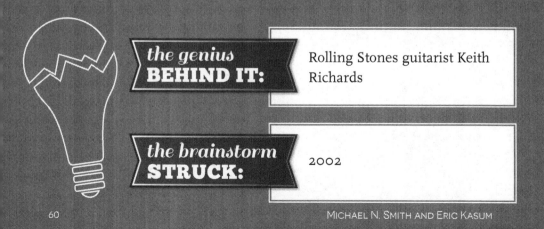

bring on the BLUNDER:

Legendary wild-child rocker Keith Richards, by his own admission, has inhaled an elephant's trunk full of illicit substances over the past four decades. But his confession to a British magazine takes getting high to a new low.

Shortly after his father Bert's death, Richards admits to mixing his cremated dad's ashes with cocaine—and snorting the morbid concoction up his nose.

from bad TO WORSE:

Not surprisingly, public revulsion follows his bizarre revelation. In way of explanation, an unrepentant Richards responds: "I couldn't resist. My father wouldn't have cared."

Rating the high he got from dad's remains, he boasts: "It went down pretty well. And I'm still alive."

dumb LUCK:

Later, upon reflection, Richards admonishes young musicians against adopting his hard-partying, carnal-delighting, turn-your-face-into-a-fright-mask brand of living, shrugging: "I've just been lucky."

after THOUGHTS:

Of his own mortality, Richards sardonically opines: "I was number one on the 'who's likely to die' list for ten years. I mean, I was really disappointed when I finally fell off the list."

COUSIN EDDIE CHECKS IN,
but He Doesn't CHECK OUT

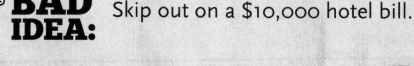

the BAD IDEA: Skip out on a $10,000 hotel bill.

the genius BEHIND IT:

Actor Randy Quaid

the brainstorm STRUCK:

June 2008

bring on the BLUNDER:

"I don't know why they call it Hamburger Helper. We like it just fine without the hamburger," states actor Randy Quaid's ne'er-do-well alter ego, Cousin Eddie, in the 1983 summer comedy *National Lampoon's Vacation*.

But it's clear from Randy and wife Evi's gaudy $10,000 lodging-and-room-service tab, rung up during a brief stay at the exclusive San Ysidro Ranch in Santa Barbara, California, that the actor's tastes lean more in the direction of *Caviar* Helper. All of which is fine except for one last detail the Oscar-nominated star of *The Last Detail* ignores: paying his bill.

from bad **TO WORSE:**

Meanwhile, back at the ranch, tempers flair. Unable to collect from the Quaids after weeks of trying, the hotel successfully implores the DA to press criminal charges for felony fraud and conspiracy. Still, the couple decides to skip five voluntary court dates—all the while fighting with its legal team.

Frustrated, a Santa Barbara judge sends police to remand the couple into custody. Evi resists arrest, then posts bail and parks a large truck on a main local thoroughfare adorned with a hand-painted sign accusing her arresting officer of taking bribes. The officer sues for defamation.

dumb **LUCK:**

Following months of legal wrangling and wild-eyed accusations, the Quaids finally have their day in court. In a bizarre plea for leniency, the handcuffed actor holds out his Golden Globe Award, won in 1988 for *LBJ: The Early Years*, and forlornly tells the judge: "See? I used to be a winner." Upon showing proof of payment of their hotel bill, Randy has his charges dropped. But Evi's not so lucky. She's sentenced to 240 hours of community service.

after **THOUGHTS:**

The Quaids' strange behavior first surfaces during a 2008 payment dispute with an Actors' Equity employee, who claims the couple threatened "We're going to get you," while calling the worker "a Nazi bitch." A Los Angeles judge grants Actors' Equity a restraining order against the Quaids days later.

DR. DUDE LITTLE

the BAD IDEA: Offer to give a ride to a "woman" staggering down Santa Monica Boulevard at 4 a.m.

the genius BEHIND IT: Funnyman Eddie Murphy

the brainstorm STRUCK: May 2, 1997

bring on the BLUNDER:

Tossing and turning one sleepless Thursday night, actor/comedian Eddie Murphy decides to drive his wife's SUV to a nearby West Hollywood newsstand to browse the latest periodicals.

On his way back home, the star of the soon-to-premiere *Dr. Doolittle* encounters a diminutive damsel in distress. He notices her "having a problem," stumbling down a tough section of Santa Monica Boulevard. In a moment of compassion (or abject stupidity), Murphy pulls over, throws open the passenger-side door, and offers to give her a ride.

MICHAEL N. SMITH AND ERIC KASUM

from bad TO WORSE:

Two miles down the road, the *Beverly Hills Cop* jokester is surprised to be pulled over by an unmarked LA County Sheriff's vice squad car. The deputies accost Murphy with two rather disturbing bits of information: First, his passenger is no damsel—he's a dude named Atisone Seiuli, twenty, of Los Angeles. Second, he's a transvestite hooker with outstanding warrants for prostitution.

dumb LUCK:

Seiuli goes on record claiming that, during their brief sport-utility sojourn, Murphy handed him two $100 bills and asked: "Can I see you in lingerie?" "What kind of sex do you like?" and various questions about Seiuli's feet.

Putting his worst foot forward, Murphy's cross-dressing hitchhiker is arrested for violating probation on the earlier prostitution conviction. Insisting he was just giving Seiuli a "good Samaritan" ride, Murphy is not charged.

after THOUGHTS:

In 2005, implying that hubby Eddie was less interested in getting a newspaper than getting off, wife Nicole references the prostitute pickup fiasco in an attempt to void the couple's prenuptial agreement during contentious divorce proceedings.

"He told me there was this person on the corner crying, so he stopped to help. But I'm thinking, 'Well, why the hell did you let him get into the car?'" The Murphys' divorce is finalized in 2006.

Five of the Worst Ideas in Presidential History

The geniuses behind it: Various U.S. presidents
The brainstorm struck: 1875 to 2003

Bad idea 1875: Lord, Grant Him the Wisdom.

As a military leader, he's the stuff of legend. As an evaluator of political appointees, he's a stuffed shirt. Hero of the North's victory in the Civil War, President Ulysses S. Grant may have been the worst judge of character in chief executive history.

His choice for Treasury Secretary, William Richardson, is caught taking kickbacks from a tax collector. The infamous "Whiskey Ring" implicates Grant's private secretary in an alcohol-tax-fraud scheme. His Secretary of the Interior allegedly accepts bribes to secure land deals—while his Secretary of the Navy is accused of receiving secret payoffs from defense contractors. In all, eleven scandals rock his two terms in office, sullying his previously stellar reputation forever.

Bad idea 1928: The Great Deregulation.

A firm believer in the primacy of big business and the fecklessness of government, Republican president Herbert Hoover champions deregulation of Wall Street and laissez-faire economic policy. The Great Depression follows quickly thereafter (along with twenty consecutive years of Democratic presidents once Hoover's ousted from office).

Bad idea 1964: Guns and Butter.

Presidents Eisenhower and Kennedy believe that the conflict in Vietnam merits no more U.S. involvement than can be handled by a few military advisors. President Lyndon Johnson thinks otherwise. He ups the ante and commits over 530,000 troops to Vietnam by 1968. At the same time, he introduces sea-changing new social programs, such as Social Security and Medicaid. Result: Over 58,000 Americans die in this war of choice. And the costly, concurrent social and military initiatives help plunge the United States into the deep recession of the 1970s.

Bad idea 1984: One Big Contra-Diction.

The Nicaraguan Contras fighting the Cuban-backed Sandinistas are, to President Ronald Reagan, "Freedom Fighters"—in some ways "the moral equivalent of our Founding Fathers." But the Boland Amendment prohibits our CIA and Defense Department from supporting those rebel forces. After vowing never to negotiate with terrorists, Reagan contradicts his own directive by selling arms to Iran in exchange for the release of three of seven American hostages they hold. Cash from the sale is then diverted, off the books, to fund the Contras. Fourteen people are later charged with crimes. And the president's image of honesty and integrity is compromised.

Bad idea 2000: Never Recount Yourself Out.

Democratic candidate Al Gore wins the popular vote in the 2000 presidential election by more than 500,000 votes. But he loses the Electoral College tally—and therefore the election—271 to 266 to Republican George W. Bush. The Gore campaign decides to challenge the vote count in Florida, in four key Democratic-leaning counties. A recount ensues. The U.S. Supreme Court then stops the recount, contending that it violates the equal protection clause of the U.S. Constitution by focusing on some—rather than all—of the state's ballots. With that, Bush is declared the winner. But if Gore's lawyers had asked for a recount of all votes cast in the state, no violation of the equal protection clause could have been claimed. And by some recount analyses, Gore might have won Florida—and therefore the entire election.

INEPT
INVENTIONS
PITIFUL
PRODUCTS,
& SENSELESS
SERVICES

THE BUTT *of* a FAT JOKE

the BAD IDEA: Olestra.

the geniuses BEHIND IT: Procter & Gamble food-additive scientists

the brainstorm STRUCK: 1968

bring on the BLUNDER: Since the dawn of our republic, Americans have been wrestling with a great existential question: "How can I shove limitless fistfuls of fatty snack foods into my bloated face without making my arteries harder than last week's linguine?"

Finally, in 1968, P&G discovers the answer: Olestra. Thanks to this new chemically contrived fat substitute, we can now consume vast quantities of potato chips, cookies, crackers, and more—fat-free and worry-free. But (or should we say "butt"?), there's a particularly unappetizing problem.

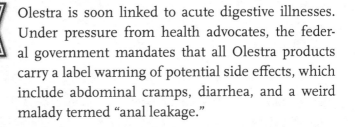

from bad TO WORSE: Olestra is soon linked to acute digestive illnesses. Under pressure from health advocates, the federal government mandates that all Olestra products carry a label warning of potential side effects, which include abdominal cramps, diarrhea, and a weird malady termed "anal leakage."

dumb LUCK: After an initial surge of public acceptance, Olestra product sales drop by 50 percent within two years. More than 20,000 consumer health complaints are lodged. And the additive's early promise of delivering guiltless, healthy snack foods becomes a big, fat joke.

after THOUGHTS: Today, Olestra is used as an ingredient in deck-staining products and machine lubricants. Yum! While banned in the United Kingdom and Canada, it can still be found under the brand name Olean in some American snack foods.

A KILLER IDEA *for* SAVING LIVES

the **BAD IDEA:** Set out to save the lives of soldiers by inventing a better way to kill them.

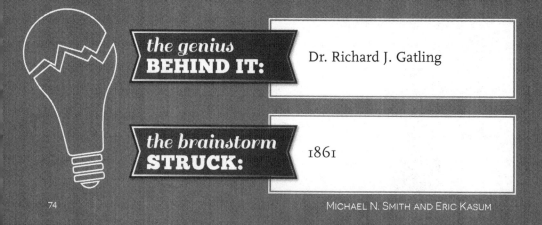

the genius **BEHIND IT:** Dr. Richard J. Gatling

the brainstorm **STRUCK:** 1861

bring on the BLUNDER:

About the same time Louis Pasteur is pioneering disease prevention through milk pasteurization, Dr. Richard Gatling is pondering a strangely different strategy for improving human health and longevity: Invent a better killing machine.

Disturbed by the internecine carnage of America's deadliest conflict—the still-raging Civil War—Gatling sets out to create a gun that by its very rapid-fire efficiency will enable one soldier to do the work of an entire battalion. The need for large armies, he counterintuitively reasons, would be eliminated, thereby diminishing the aggregate death and destruction of this—or any—war.

from bad TO WORSE:

A far cry from the old single-shot musket, Gatling's prototype "machine gun" fires an unprecedented 350 bullets per minute. Later in the Civil War, the Union army adds the weapon to its arsenal—with devastating effects—helping to push the Confederacy into reluctant surrender.

dumb LUCK:

The British in Egypt, the Russians in central Asia, and the United States in the Spanish-American War utilize the machine gun to pile up massive enemy casualties. Altruistically conceived to curb battle fatalities, Gatling's amazing weapon instead spawns burgeoning death tolls in dozens of conflicts worldwide.

after THOUGHTS:

With the switch to smaller, lighter weaponry, Gatling guns fall out of favor in the early twentieth century. Yet their ability to maintain continuous fire without overheating has since fueled a resurgence. Today, "Gatlings" can be found on A-10 Thunderbolt II Warthog aircraft and a variety of attack helicopters.

The PINHEAD INVENTOR WHO NEVER GOT the POINT

the BAD IDEA: Invent what becomes one of the world's most popular devices, then quickly sell its patent rights for next to nothing.

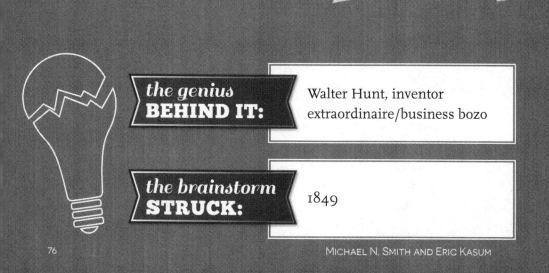

the genius BEHIND IT: Walter Hunt, inventor extraordinaire/business bozo

the brainstorm STRUCK: 1849

MICHAEL N. SMITH AND ERIC KASUM

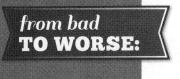

bring on the BLUNDER: An inventor since his teen years, Hunt is Superman when it comes to conjuring up revolutionary innovations: the sewing machine, the fountain pen, and the repeating rifle, among others. But he's kryptonite when it comes to business. So, while he putters, others profit from the products he creates.

from bad TO WORSE: One day, while bending and shaping a common piece of wire, Hunt fashions a revolutionary new device: the safety pin.

He wisely patents his sharp idea. Cash-strapped, he then unwisely sells the patent rights hours later to W. R. Grace & Co. for a mere $400.

dumb LUCK: The safety pin—offering a safer clasp for baby diapers and clothing than traditional straight pins—becomes an essential product in American homes and businesses, earning W. R. Grace untold millions over the years on their meager $400 investment.

after THOUGHTS: The Singer Sewing Company in 1858 agrees to pay Hunt the then-enormous sum of $50,000 for his sewing machine design. Taking his financial hard luck to the grave, Hunt dies a few months later—before Singer can make a single payment.

OCTOBOMB

BLANK 8-TRACK
CARTRIDGE

45 min.
total time
@ 3¾ i.p.s

the BAD IDEA:

The eight-track cassette tape.

the geniuses BEHIND IT: The audiophiles at RCA Victor, Motorola, Ampex, Ford, General Motors, and Lear Jet

the brainstorm STRUCK: 1964

In the frantic quest for a handy, durable, high-fidelity tape format suitable for playing recorded music in automobiles, a consortium of top automotive and electronics manufacturers make a startling choice: They decide to consult a madman.

Inspired by Earl "Madman" Muntz, known for his wild antics as a TV pitchman and developer of the continuous-loop Stereo-Pak tape cartridge, the group advances a new music delivery system: the eight-track cassette. And while that sounds good on paper, eight-track tape, unfortunately, sounds bad in automobiles.

from bad TO WORSE:

First, audio aficionados complain that eight-track tape hiss reduces sound quality. Strike two: Eight-track cassettes often change tracks in the middle of a song resulting in musicus interruptus.

Also, annoyingly, eight-track cassettes can't be rewound. To hear your favorite tune on a given album, you just have to wait until it comes around again. Worse, eight-tracks are expensive—especially when compared to newly introduced compact cassette tapes.

dumb LUCK:

Though briefly popular in the 1970s, eight-tracks are soon eclipsed by smaller, cheaper, click-free, rewindable compact cassettes—and later by compact discs. By the late 1980s, the format fizzles out of production, a relic of the polyester era.

after THOUGHTS:

Fleetwood Mac's Greatest Hits, released in November 1988, is regarded as the last commercial eight-track album by a major label. A small but avid group of collectors keeps the format alive today.

THEY BET *on* *the* PONIES AND LOST

the **BAD IDEA:**

The Pony Express.

the geniuses **BEHIND IT:**

William H. Russell, William B. Waddell, and Alexander Majors

the brainstorm **STRUCK:**

January 1860

bring on the BLUNDER:

With the Civil War looming, business partners Russell, Waddell, and Majors astutely foresee the need to speed vital communication more rapidly across the burgeoning American frontier.

But rather than invest in the nascent field of electronic messaging, the trio of rugged individualists decides to place its money on good old-fashioned horsepower—establishing the legendary mail delivery enterprise called the Pony Express. And although the company is well stocked with horseshoes, the venture proves anything but a lucky bet.

from bad TO WORSE:

Traversing the 2,000-mile trail from St. Joseph, Missouri to Sacramento, California, the average 125-pound Pony Express rider delivers a 20-pound sack of mail in just under ten days (changing riders every seventy-five to one hundred miles). The charge: $5 postage for a single letter.

Here's the problem: The new transcontinental telegraph is wiring its way across the nation with the power to dispatch messages in mere moments for pennies. Upon transmitting its first dots, the telegraph quickly dashes the hopes of a successful Pony Express.

dumb LUCK:

After only nineteen months of operation—and the equivalent of millions of dollars in losses—the Pony Express heads for that great stable in the sky. Its founders file for bankruptcy.

after THOUGHTS:

These days, you can send a letter across the country for a mere forty-nine cents. That's chicken feed (as opposed to horse feed) compared to the $5 fee ($100 in today's money) the Pony Express charged for the same service.

THIS GAME REALLY STICKS OUT IN YOUR MIND

the BAD IDEA: Create a backyard game that requires children to throw large, heavy, pointed metallic darts high into the air.

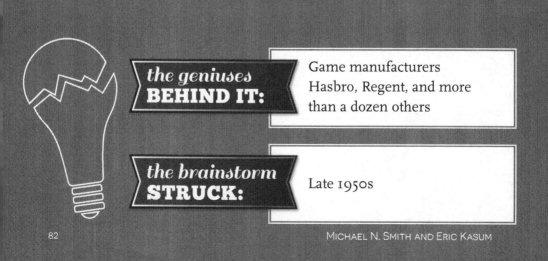

the geniuses BEHIND IT: Game manufacturers Hasbro, Regent, and more than a dozen others

the brainstorm STRUCK: Late 1950s

MICHAEL N. SMITH AND ERIC KASUM

bring on the BLUNDER:

What would you call an outdoor game where one player heaves a weighted, foot-long, metal-tipped dart skyward, hoping to land and stick it in the middle of a plastic hoop placed at the feet of his opponent some twenty feet away? You'd call it "lawn darts," "Jarts," "garden darts"—or maybe just "the most idiotically dangerous kids' game ever invented."

from bad TO WORSE:

Amid all the family outing, picnic-time, lawn-dart fun, three children are gruesomely—if unsurprisingly—impaled and killed by the large airborne darts in the 1960s and 1970s. Over 6,000 more are seriously injured—most of them under ten years of age. Their lethal qualities now manifested, lawn darts are used as weapons in a 1980 Post Falls, Idaho, gang murder.

dumb LUCK:

Citing these deaths and numerous injuries, the Consumer Product Safety Commission bans lawn darts from sale in the United States in 1988. The following year, their sale is also banned in Canada. Today, lawn dart purchases are still forbidden—even on eBay.

after THOUGHTS:

Each of the past seventeen years, Bellefontaine, Ohio, has played host to an annual Jarts tournament, sporting a $300 first prize. Underground sources of the cult-popular game can still be found on the Internet.

A DUMB WAY to TEST HOW SMART YOU ARE

the BAD IDEA:

The IQ test.

the genius BEHIND IT:
French psychologist Alfred Binet

the brainstorm STRUCK:
1911

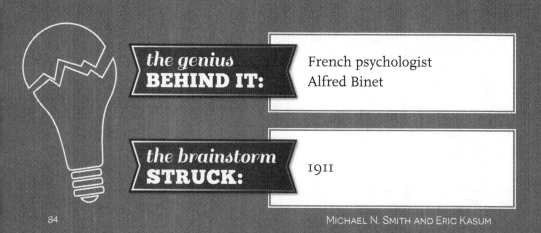

MICHAEL N. SMITH AND ERIC KASUM

While his cousin Charles Darwin theorizes on the origins of the human species, British scientist Frances Galton theorizes on the origins of human intelligence—and posits that such intelligence is measurable.

With Galton's hypotheses in hand, Alfred Binet and Stanford psychologist Lewis Terman create the Stanford-Binet Intelligence Quotient. It's the first human intelligence test. And although widely embraced, critics nonetheless declare it to be IQ: Incomplete and Questionable.

**from bad
TO WORSE:**

The main complaint: the IQ test covers only reasoning, vocabulary, and problem solving. Creativity is not considered. Intuition is not evaluated. Originality, humor, verbal aptitude—many of the characteristics of intellects—are not assessed. Therefore opponents claim that IQ is a weak (if not false) indicator of true intelligence and future achievement.

**dumb
LUCK:**

"Intelligence is a much more complex thing than what the test measures," reasons Dr. Morton Beiser of the University of Toronto.

Furthermore, psychologist Howard Gardner of Harvard, a pioneer in the research of "interpersonal intelligence" (social skills) and "intrapersonal intelligence" (knowing one's self), notes that IQ tests measure neither and therefore are not the most intelligent ways to evaluate intelligence.

**after
THOUGHTS:**

Despite its shortcomings, the IQ test, an industrial-age relic, remains the most highly regarded indicator of intelligence today.

RACIALLY INSENSITIVE RESTAURANT SERVES UP
a *Side of* CONTROVERSY

the BAD IDEA: Name your restaurant chain after a derogatory term for African Americans.

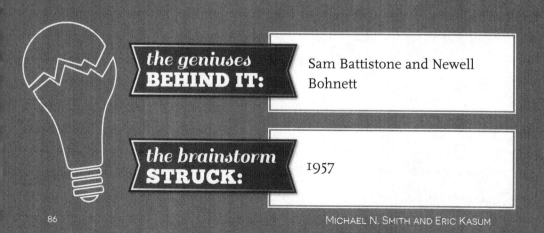

the geniuses BEHIND IT: Sam Battistone and Newell Bohnett

the brainstorm STRUCK: 1957

MICHAEL N. SMITH AND ERIC KASUM

bring on the BLUNDER:

Just about everyone in sleepy, seaside Santa Barbara, California, knows restaurateur Sam Battistone as good old "Sam." His partner, Newell Bohnett, is affectionately nicknamed "Bo." So when the men get together to open a restaurant, they decide to mash their names together and dub their glorified coffee shop "Sambo's."

Innocent enough, it seems. Well, except when you consider that African Americans have been derided with the racist slang "sambo" since the publication of *The Story of Little Black Sambo* in 1899.

from bad TO WORSE:

Unwilling to leave bad enough alone, Sam and Bo opt to capitalize on the book's notoriety by decorating their restaurant chain with the image of a dark-skinned boy frolicking with tigers in the jungle.

It's the late 1970s. Now with twelve hundred units in forty-seven states, the restaurant behemoth is buffeted by protests from civil rights groups—who find Sambo's name and imagery (which they claim characterizes blacks as lazy and childlike) demeaning.

dumb LUCK:

Ownership reacts by renaming some of its restaurants "the Jolly Tiger." In 1981, others are renamed "No Place Like Sam's." But company profits are melting faster than butter on a hotcake. The chain files for bankruptcy. And by 1982, all but the original Sambo's are closed for good.

after THOUGHTS:

Also the first owner of the NBA's New Orleans Jazz, Sam Battistone leaves his restaurant legacy to his grandson, restaurateur Chad Stevens, who today operates that one remaining Sambo's, in Santa Barbara.

NEW COKE'S
PRODUCT LAUNCH GOES
from FIZZY *to* FLAT

the BAD IDEA: Change the flavor formula of the world's most popular soft drink.

the geniuses BEHIND IT:

Senior executives of the Coca-Cola Company

the brainstorm STRUCK:

1985

bring on the BLUNDER:

In the bubbly affluence of post–World War II America, Coke is the cola preferred by 60 percent of the market. Yet by 1983, pesky rival Pepsi has begun to outsell Coke among coveted youth demographics. As Coke's market share sinks to 24 percent, Coke CEO Roberto Goizueta orders a rethinking of the company's operations. Even Coke's century-old secret formula is reevaluated. Despite a generations-long reign as the world's top-selling soft drink, "The Real Thing"—a bastion of coolheaded product stability now sweating in the heat of competition—is ready to change its taste.

Coke researchers fan out across America armed with trial samples of New Coke, a slightly sweeter, more Pepsi-like take on the soda's traditional flavor.

In blind taste tests, consumers choose New Coke over traditional Coke and Pepsi by wide margins. In focus groups, though, New Coke is met with far less enthusiasm. Still, Coke management, thirsty for a winner, launches "the new taste of Coca-Cola" to mark the company's centennial celebration in 1985. Public reaction, especially among Coke loyalists, immediately moves from fizzy to flat.

dumb
LUCK:

Within days, the company receives over 400,000 distraught calls and angry letters. A psychiatrist retained to evaluate the tenor of calls from consumers states that they sound like people mourning the death of a loved one. Even Fidel Castro criticizes the move as another example of "American decadence."

With boycotts looming—just three months after its historic birth—New Coke is history. Traditionally formulated Coke, now termed "Coca-Cola Classic," is reintroduced. And after hundreds of millions of dollars spent testing and marketing New Coke, executives conclude that they had simply underestimated the public's "deep and abiding emotional attachment" to the original.

after
THOUGHTS:

By late 1985, Coca-Cola Classic substantially outsells New Coke and Pepsi, solidifying its number-one-soft-drink status that continues to this day—prompting some conspiracy buffs to contend that New Coke was simply a clever scheme to boost sales of original Coke all along.

The PUBIC HAIRPIECE

the BAD IDEA:

Wear a hairpiece over your lousy private parts.

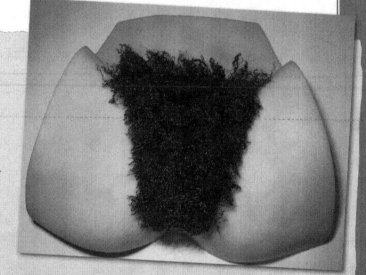

the geniuses BEHIND IT: European prostitutes

the brainstorm STRUCK: 1617

MICHAEL N. SMITH AND ERIC KASUM

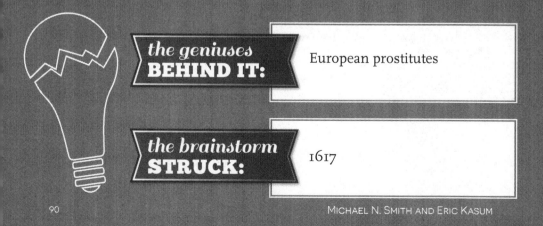

bring on the BLUNDER:

Seventeenth-century hookers have a pubic problem that's gone public. Doing the nasty with numerous lice-ridden sailors, farmers, vagrants, and sundry dirty scoundrels has left parasites o'plenty in the working girls' privates. And that's proving to be bad for business.

So, in an effort to deny the pesky lice their densely forested base of operation, the prostitutes shave their pubic hair. Then, in order to hide that fact from their johns, many wear a pubis-mounted hairpiece known as a "merkin."

from bad TO WORSE:

Now, while merkins may be good at disguising a given prostitute's creepy-crawly crotch, they do nothing to eliminate the original infestation. Hence, the parasites find new hosts and spread each time a working girl beds a new sex partner.

dumb LUCK:

What's more, merkins themselves become havens for bacteria and other parasites, making them as problematic as the original pubic hair they replace. Even worse, merkins obscure evidence of syphilis, one of the great deadly scourges of the era.

after THOUGHTS:

Today, merkins—single-use, disposable, and *far* more sanitary—are worn by film actors and actresses to prevent inadvertent exposure of their genitalia during nude or seminude scenes.

WD-528,000,000,000

the BAD IDEA:

Sell your rights to a product that eventually generates over $500 billion in cash flow for a mere $10,000.

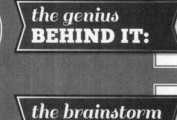

the genius **BEHIND IT:**
Norman B. Larsen, investor/chemist

the brainstorm **STRUCK:**
Mid-1950s

MICHAEL N. SMITH AND ERIC KASUM

The relentless Larsen and his tiny Rocket Chemical Company try thirty-nine different formulas aimed at protecting the outer skin of America's Atlas rocket from moisture-borne corrosion. On their 40th try, RCC's squeaky wheels get the oil, discovering a versatile recipe called WD-40: WD to connote "water dispersing" and 40 to commemorate their 40th attempt to get it right.

Boasting the intellect of a world-class inventor—combined with the intuition of a third-rate businessman—Larsen sells his interest in the fledgling WD-40 operation for a paltry $10,000, positing that he could always invent something better.

from bad
TO WORSE:

Soon, RCC employees begin to find common household uses for the product. Its nonvolatile hydrocarbon formula is ideal for lubricating hinges, loosening screws and bolts, removing adhesives, and hundreds of other imaginative applications.

In 1958, WD-40 appears in San Diego–area stores. By 1960, the company doubles in size. Thirteen years later, the renamed WD-40 Company goes public. Its stock price skyrockets 61 percent. By 1993, four out of five American households are purchasing a combined one million cans of this astonishing product each week.

dumb
LUCK:

Today, the company Norman Larsen sold for bubkes has a market value of $528 billion dollars.

after
THOUGHTS:

Though he never tops the success of his WD-40 formulation, Larsen keeps inventing, eventually creating Free N' Kleen, which he considers superior to WD-40. But shortly after his untimely death at age forty-seven, Free N' Kleen goes out of business.

POLITICALLY INCORRECT POLITICOS

MONKEY BUSINESS SINKS *a* PRESIDENTIAL CAMPAIGN

the BAD IDEA:
Dare the media to catch you engaging in an extramarital affair.

the genius BEHIND IT:

Senator Gary Hart

the brainstorm STRUCK:

1987

bring on the BLUNDER:

On the heels of surprisingly effective showings in the 1984 Democratic presidential primaries, a little-known U.S. senator from Colorado, Gary Hart, emerges as the new surefire nominee in the run-up to the 1988 campaign.

But on the road to the nomination, Hart's character is assailed by eyebrow-raising revelations: that he's quietly changed his last name from Hartpence; that he claims to be a year younger than his birth certificate shows; that he's altered his signature repeatedly throughout his adult life; and that he's separated from his wife three different times.

Declared a flake and a womanizer by his adversaries, Hart fights back rumors that he's embarked on an extramarital affair, daring the press corps to: "Follow me around. I don't care. If anybody wants to put a tail on me, go ahead. They'll be very bored."

Two reporters from the *Miami Herald* take him up on his challenge. Staking out Hart's Washington townhouse, they report observing a young woman leave the premises on the evening of May 2. Days later, a photo emerges of the same woman, Donna Rice, sitting on Hart's lap after an outing aboard the aptly named yacht *Monkey Business.* With his poll numbers sinking faster than the boat's anchor, a chastened Hart quickly withdraws his candidacy the following week.

dumb
LUCK:

In December 1987, riding a renewed rush of populist zeal, Hart vows to "let the people decide" and returns to the race. The people, it seems, have decided: Hart garners a dispiriting 4 percent of the New Hampshire primary vote. For the last time, Gary Hart exits presidential politics.

after
THOUGHTS:

Although he never again holds public office, Hart earns a doctorate from Oxford in 2001—and in 2006 accepts an endowed professorship at the University of Colorado at Denver. Some political commentators note that his sexual indiscretions—coupled with revelations of former president John F. Kennedy's extramarital affairs—helped soften Americans' attitudes on the subject (for example, by turning public opinion against convicting President Bill Clinton of impeachment following his dalliance with former intern Monica Lewinsky in the late 1990s).

TAPE CREATES
a STICKY SITUATION *for*
TRICKY DICK

the BAD IDEA:

While burglarizing the Democratic National Committee office, use thick, easy-to-spot duct tape to keep the entry door unlatched.

the genius **BEHIND IT:**

Electronics expert, former CIA agent, and Watergate henchman James W. McCord Jr.

the brainstorm **STRUCK:**

June 17, 1972

bring on the BLUNDER:

Ranking members of President Richard M. Nixon's reelection committee get a tip that his opponent, Democratic presidential candidate George S. McGovern, may have received illegal campaign contributions from benefactors in communist Cuba.

On that news, Nixon campaign operative G. Gordon Liddy springs into action. He enlists McCord and five other men to break into Democratic National Committee headquarters in Washington's Watergate complex to see what evidence of a McGovern/Cuba connection they can find.

from bad TO WORSE:

On a June night in 1972, a security guard at Watergate notices that the latch on the door leading to the DNC HQ has been taped open. He removes the tape and continues on his rounds. An hour later, he notices that the door has been retaped—evidence that an intruder is in the building. He quickly calls the police.

dumb LUCK:

The burglars—and later Liddy—are arrested. And McCord soon implicates members of the Nixon administration in the crime. A common piece of tape has opened the door to Watergate, the most infamous government scandal of the century.

after THOUGHTS:

Audio tape is not Nixon's friend either. Recordings of Nixon's Oval Office conversations help link his administration to a cover-up of the break-in—leading to the impeachment and resignation of the president on August 9, 1974.

The GRAND HIGH EXALTED HOO-HAH *of* THE UNITED STATES

the BAD IDEA:

Mandate that the president of the United States carry the official title of "His Elective Majesty."

JOHN ADAMS,
SECOND PRESIDENT OF THE UNITED STATES.
PHILADELPHIA.

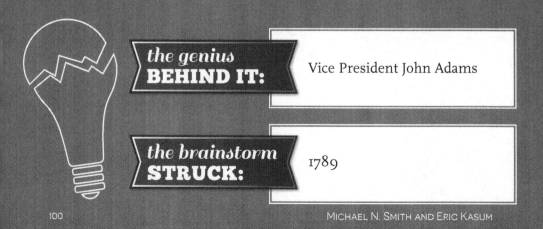

the genius BEHIND IT: Vice President John Adams

the brainstorm STRUCK: 1789

MICHAEL N. SMITH AND ERIC KASUM

bring on the BLUNDER:

A bulwark of the American Revolution and a clarion voice for the adoption of our nation's Declaration of Independence from "the tyranny of the British monarchy," Vice President John Adams curiously decides to champion a quintessentially un-American idea.

As one of our Founding Fathers, he feels a deep antipathy toward the highfalutin aristocrats of Europe. Yet he believes that a leader of the newly formed United States, in order to be perceived as an equal among the kings and queens ruling much of the civilized world, requires a title more regal than the functional, prosaic "President of the United States."

from bad TO WORSE:

At his urging, the fledgling Congress debates the concept of what to call our country's chief executive. One proposal: "His Excellency the President of the United States." Another interesting entry: "His Highness the President of the United States of America and Protector of the Rights of Same." Adams himself fancies such soaring appellations as "His Majesty the President" and "His High Mightiness."

dumb LUCK:

After a month of often-heated debate, the legislators come to their senses, settling on a simple, basic title: "President of the United States." Ironically, a mere eight years later, Adams himself will answer to that designation as America's second commander in chief.

after THOUGHTS:

At the height of the great presidential name debate, one frustrated congressman, sarcastically commenting on Adams's portliness, refers to the vice president as "His Rotundity."

A TURKEY *of* AN IDEA GETS PLUCKED

the BAD IDEA:

Reschedule Thanksgiving.

the genius **BEHIND IT:**	President Franklin D. Roosevelt

| *the brainstorm* **STRUCK:** | 1939 |

Michael N. Smith and Eric Kasum

As the Great Depression lingers on, President Roosevelt and his advisors have a shiny new concept for boosting the lackluster U.S. economy: Move Thanksgiving from late November to seven days earlier in the month.

That way, they reason, Christmas shoppers will have one more week to buy presents, thereby invigorating moribund retail sales. They're hopeful America will gladly gobble-gobble up this "minor" scheduling change.

from bad
TO WORSE:

Instead, an irate populace immediately places Roosevelt's bird-brained concept on the chopping block. Calendars will now be inaccurate, it's argued. College football games will have to be rescheduled. Aunt Marge and Uncle Lou might show up for stuffing and cranberry sauce on the wrong day. Angry letters pour into the White House.

dumb
LUCK:

Twenty-three states refuse to recognize the president's new Thanksgiving date. Texas and Colorado decide to celebrate the new Thanksgiving Day—and the old one too! The following year, Roosevelt apologetically returns the holiday to its original day.

after
THOUGHTS:

Congress later passes legislation setting Thanksgiving as the final Thursday in November. Never again will this turkey of an idea be allowed to fly.

MAIL *to the* CHIEF

the BAD IDEA: Refuse to accept any mail deliveries marked "postage due."

the genius **BEHIND IT:** The penny-unwise General Zachary Taylor

the brainstorm **STRUCK:** 1848

MICHAEL N. SMITH AND ERIC KASUM

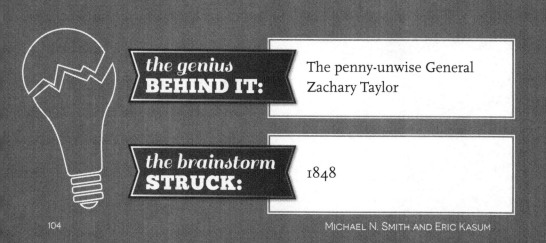

A grizzled forty-year veteran of America's wars against Britain, American Indians, and Mexico, General Zachary Taylor is the quintessential rugged individualist of frontier lore. Well-wishers from across the young nation send Old Rough and Ready hundreds of fan letters—many with unpaid postage due, a common practice in these days.

But the cost-conscious curmudgeon instructs the local postmaster to hold all such letters, declaring he'll not a pay a cent of postage to have the ego-burnishing missives delivered.

**from bad
TO WORSE:**

Alas, pinching pennies proves costly. Because Taylor has captured the surprise nomination of the Whig Party for president, notice of which is sent by letter from the party convention—sent, yes, with postage due.

The Whigs get no response from their nominee. Weeks pass. At last, the general's associates read a newspaper story heralding his mailed nomination. Only then does the recipient retrieve the letter, pay the postage due, and formally agree to run for president.

**dumb
LUCK:**

Having won the 1848 election, now-president Taylor dines in celebration, sampling dishes prepared by local townspeople. But some observers darkly speculate that his food has been laced with arsenic.

**after
THOUGHTS:**

Though no conclusive evidence of poisoning is ever found, Taylor tragically dies of gastroenteritis shortly thereafter—just sixteen months after taking office.

The **BRIDGE** to **NOWHERE**

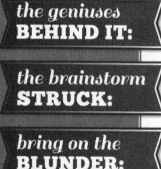

the geniuses BEHIND IT:

Alaska's senator Ted Stevens, representative Don Young, and governor Sarah Palin

the brainstorm STRUCK:

2005

bring on the BLUNDER:

As hundreds of thousands of wind-whipped, rain-drenched, homeless and hungry Louisiana residents plead for federal assistance in the devastating aftermath of Hurricane Katrina, DC power brokers are busy focusing on what is, at the moment, the U.S. government's top priority: providing about fifty Alaska residents a multimillion-dollar bridge connecting their remote island town to the mainland.

from bad TO WORSE:

Washington waste watchdogs and media commentators soon dub the Golden Gate–sized boondoggle a $398-million "Bridge to Nowhere"—an enormous, fatty cut of government pork serving a sparse few at a time of great need for many.

Still, wielding righteous indignation, Alaska senator Ted Stevens, Governor Sarah Palin, and other state politicos turn a blind eye to the Katrina calamity, dig their mukluks into the tundra, and refuse to budge on the bridge-funding request.

dumb LUCK:

Although Gravina Island is home to Ketchikan International Airport, even the most optimistic reports project the controversial bridge will carry only 950 people per day. (The aforementioned Golden Gate Bridge, by contrast, carries about 120,000 each day.)

With national ridicule building, Senator Tom Coburn of Oklahoma introduces a proposal to recoup $223 million already appropriated for the Alaskan span and reallocate it to Katrina relief efforts. Despite Senator Stevens's threat to quit the Senate if the funds are revoked, Congress redirects his cherished bridge bucks to Louisiana. As a result, the bridge project, to this day, has gone nowhere.

after THOUGHTS:

Governor Palin's support for the bridge becomes an issue during her unsuccessful vice presidential run in 2008. Senator Stevens, amid unrelated federal corruption charges, loses his forty-year-old Senate seat in the same 2008 election. He dies in a plane crash in 2010.

MAKE YOUR MEETING
or else
MEET YOUR MAKER

the
BAD
IDEA:

Postpone a meeting between President William McKinley and inventor/garment-maker Casimir Zeglen.

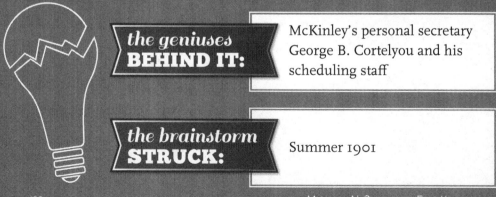

the geniuses **BEHIND IT:**	McKinley's personal secretary George B. Cortelyou and his scheduling staff

the brainstorm **STRUCK:**	Summer 1901

Michael N. Smith and Eric Kasum

bring on the BLUNDER:

Newly reelected and embarking on a national speaking tour, McKinley is a busy chief executive—too busy, Cortelyou and the president's staff decide, to meet with Zeglen, who's offered to fit the commander in chief with a snazzy piece of outerwear.

Instead, Cortelyou and his people delay the meeting until after McKinley returns from a trip to the Pan-American Exposition in Buffalo, New York.

from bad TO WORSE:

At the exposition, McKinley is confronted by angry anarchist Leon Czolgosz, who raises a handgun concealed in a handkerchief and shoots the president in the chest and abdomen. Eight days later, McKinley is dead.

dumb LUCK:

Shortly thereafter, a member of McKinley's staff recalls the postponed meeting. At that meeting, it's recalled, Zeglen was to outfit McKinley with his groundbreaking invention: the bulletproof vest. A delayed appointment helped trigger the assassination of America's 25th president.

after THOUGHTS:

On the heels of McKinley's death, Congress officially charges the Secret Service with the physical protection of U.S. presidents.

FOR WHOM THE CITY OF BELL TOLLS

the BAD IDEA: Pay the elected officers of a small, working-class city more than the president of the United States.

the geniuses BEHIND IT: Government administrators, Bell, California

the brainstorm STRUCK: 2005

bring on the BLUNDER: In a special election that promises to ring in a new day for the 36,000-resident Southern California city of Bell, a meager four hundred people show up to vote. But that mere 1 percent of the electorate unleashes a series of events that positions this one-mile-square, largely immigrant municipality at the locus of one of the most notorious civic corruption scandals in recent American history.

MICHAEL N. SMITH AND ERIC KASUM

Energized by citizen disinterest and disengagement, Bell's conniving political class, headed by esteemed city manager Robert Rizzo, schemes to change Bell's charter—a change that quietly, cleverly would exempt him and his cronies from statewide salary restrictions. Believing Rizzo's assertion that the charter conversion will "expand local control," a ding-a-ling majority of Bell voters buy into the ruse.

Armed with this new mandate, Bell's political poo-bahs quietly award Rizzo a yearly salary of $800,000. (Barack Obama makes about half that.) His deputy manager gets $376,000 a year. The Bell police chief collects an arresting $457,000 annually. Plus, each city council member is in line to "earn" over $100,000 per annum—for a part-time position!

In 2010, the *Los Angeles Times* yanks the clapper out of the Bell scam, unleashing local and national outrage. On the heels of a poorly timed DUI arrest, Rizzo succumbs to pressure and resigns. His deputy and the police chief soon follow. City council members then vote to cut their own salaries over 90 percent (to match that of the one councilman who, unwittingly, had been receiving a more appropriate $8,000 a year all along).

Then–attorney general Jerry Brown launches criminal investigations against Rizzo and his coconspirators. Salary reform legislation is considered. And the city of Bell struggles under a mountain of debt.

Despite legal action, experts say it's likely that Rizzo and his cohorts will remain entitled to millions in pension compensation.

The President
GIVES AMERICA
the FINGER

the
BAD
IDEA:

Lie under oath.

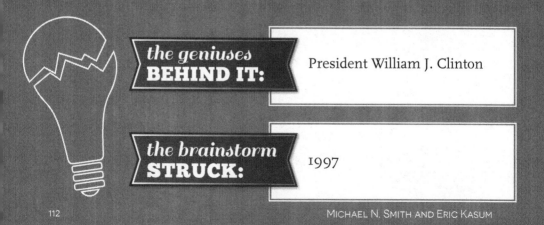

the geniuses BEHIND IT:	President William J. Clinton
the brainstorm STRUCK:	1997

MICHAEL N. SMITH AND ERIC KASUM

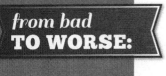

bring on the BLUNDER:

From the time of his presidential election victory in 1992, Bill Clinton is seen by his opponents as the self-indulgent, ego-driven, sex-crazed, junk-food-lusting embodiment of the Me Generation.

Despite his unquestionable intelligence (a Rhodes Scholar) and political acumen (a governor by age thirty-two), Clinton, knowing full well his enemies are out to get him, plays right into their scheming hands.

from bad TO WORSE:

He begins, in 1995, a sexual relationship with beret-wearing, thong-flashing government intern Monica Lewinsky. Word of their affair reaches Attorney General Janet Reno, who gives Special Prosecutor Ken Starr permission to expand his Whitewater real-estate-scandal investigation into the Lewinsky matter.

In response, the president takes to the airwaves, shakes his index finger at the viewing audience, and intones: "I did not have sexual relations with that woman, Miss Lewinsky." Thereafter, he denies the affair before a grand jury.

dumb LUCK:

But wait, tabloid fans. Lewinsky hands Starr indisputable evidence of her encounters with Clinton: a semen-stained frock. Fingered as a perjurer, Clinton becomes the first president since Andrew Johnson to be impeached.

after THOUGHTS:

After thirty-seven days of heated deliberation, the Senate rejects both counts of impeachment, holding that the president's conduct did not rise to "treason, bribery, or other high crimes and misdemeanors" as proscribed by the U.S. Constitution. He's later fined and loses his law license.

READ MY LIPS: NO NEW TAXES
(UNTIL I CHANGE MY MIND)

the BAD IDEA:

Base your presidential election campaign on a pledge not to raise taxes, but once in office, raise them anyway.

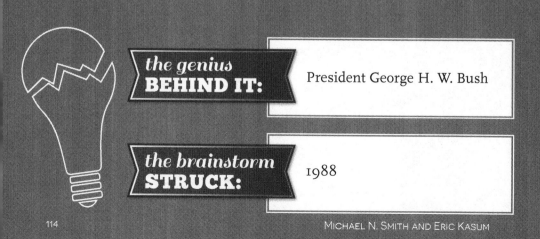

the genius BEHIND IT:	President George H. W. Bush
the brainstorm STRUCK:	1988

MICHAEL N. SMITH AND ERIC KASUM

bring on the BLUNDER:

"Politics" and "subtlety" often go together about as well as peanut butter and tuna fish. And in his run for president, Vice President George H. W. Bush is about as subtle as a crowbar to the cranium. He labels opponent Michael Dukakis "a tax and spend liberal"—and in his nomination speech burnishes his fiscal conservative street cred with the steadfast guarantee: "Read my lips: no new taxes."

Fast-forward four years: As now-president Bush prepares his reelection campaign, the nation's economy has hit the skids. Increasingly, the electorate blames the nation's financial woes on the Republican president, especially with opponent Bill Clinton relentlessly chanting the Democratic campaign mantra: "It's the economy, stupid."

from bad TO WORSE:

Looking to close the federal budget deficit and jump-start job creation, Bush gives in to the Democrat-controlled Congress and signs a new budget that, contrary to his four-year-old pledge, raises existing taxes. Conservative lip-readers are apoplectic.

dumb LUCK:

Republicans and Independents pillory Bush for reneging on his no-tax promise. With the economy tanking, the relatively unknown, though already sex-scandalized, Arkansas governor Clinton squeaks to victory with just 43 percent of the vote.

after THOUGHTS:

George H. W. Bush becomes one of only seven presidents to serve one full term and fail to win a second.

PAY NO ATTENTION TO THAT EXPLODING MOUNTAIN— JUST VOTE FOR ME

the BAD IDEA:

Urge your electorate to ignore a rumbling, smoldering volcano down the street and stick around to cast their vote.

the genius BEHIND IT: Louis Mouttet, governor of Martinique

the brainstorm STRUCK: May 7, 1902

MICHAEL N. SMITH AND ERIC KASUM

Volcano ignorance: It's that age-old affliction affecting those who cavalierly shrug off the telltale smoke wafting from a nearby mountaintop.

Which brings us to the volcano-ignorant city of St. Pierre, Martinique. See, nearby Mount Pelée has begun to rumble and smolder. Yet local governor Louis Mouttet, in a hotly contested reelection campaign (and worried that his volcano-wary electorate may split the scene), issues a somewhat self-serving civic order: "Ignore the volcano, stay put, and vote for me."

from bad TO WORSE:

To calm concerns, he issues a report stating that St. Pierre is totally safe.

But just as the report is published, hoards of poisonous snakes and insects swarm into the city, driven down the mountain by tremors and sulfurous gas. As many as fifty people die from snake and red ant bites alone.

dumb LUCK:

As Mount Pelée's ominous rumblings intensify, residents of St. Pierre finally vote to skip town. Fearing a mass exodus as election day nears, Mouttet orders troops to block the roads out of town, decreeing that the city is the safest place around in the event of an eruption.

The next day, Mount Pelée explodes in a ball of fire. In minutes, nearly all of St. Pierre's 28,000 residents, including Mouttet himself, die instantly.

after THOUGHTS:

The "all-important" election never takes place. A second eruption on May 20 obliterates what's left of the city.

Pol Pays
A HOOKER BY CHECK
and REALLY GETS SCREWED

the
BAD
IDEA:
Pay a prostitute with a seemingly harmless check.

**the genius
BEHIND IT:**

Then–Cincinnati councilman and future freak-show host, Jerry Springer

**the brainstorm
STRUCK:**

1974

**bring on the
BLUNDER:**

Faster than an unwed hillbilly mom can sock her ne'er-do-well baby daddy in the mouth, the promising political career of Jerry Springer is over.

A Northwestern University–educated lawyer, former aide to the late senator Robert F. Kennedy, and rising politico, Springer had just been elected to the Cincinnati city council at the tender age of twenty-seven when a raid on a local Kentucky massage parlor threatens to rub out his civic career.

from bad TO WORSE: In the raid, police uncover a Springer check written to the establishment (a well-known front for prostitution) to cover undefined "services." Confronted with the evidence, Springer resigns from office. Longtime Cincy newsman Al Schottelkotte pronounces the randy councilman's future political prospects limp, at best.

dumb LUCK: But not so fast, Captain Newsdude. The plucky Springer calls a press conference, fully admitting his transgression. This come-clean (so to speak) approach empowers him to win back his council seat in a landslide victory the following year.

By 1977, Springer is named mayor of Cincinnati—by the same city council that recommended his resignation three years prior. After an unsuccessful run for the Ohio governorship, the British-born Springer lands on local TV as a political/social commentator—eventually graduating to the news-anchor chair (where he is, no doubt, paid by check).

after THOUGHTS: In 1991, his serious commentaries and reportorial flourishes give way to the outlandish carnival of misfits and miscreants now familiar to all who watch the syndicated guilty pleasure known as *The Jerry Springer Show*.

THIS IS HOW I LOOK–AND I'M NOT MAKING IT UP

the BAD IDEA:

Engage in a televised presidential debate without wearing makeup.

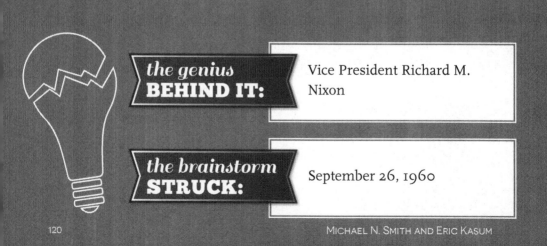

the genius BEHIND IT:
Vice President Richard M. Nixon

the brainstorm STRUCK:
September 26, 1960

MICHAEL N. SMITH AND ERIC KASUM

bring on the BLUNDER:

With the U.S. presidential election just weeks away, Vice President Nixon and Senator John F. Kennedy are running neck and neck—or should we say "face and face"?

Because on this night, their very different visages will be on display in the first presidential debate ever to be televised. And one of the candidates, lacking a firm grasp of the visual power of the relatively new medium, is about to make a fatefully dumb decision.

from bad TO WORSE:

Recently discharged from a two-week hospital stay to rehab an injured knee, Nixon, at debate time, appears pale, thin, and drawn. Sporting an ill-fitting shirt, he refuses to wear makeup, despite sunken eyes, a shiny forehead, and a darkly prominent five o'clock shadow.

Meanwhile, the future king of Camelot, fresh from a campaign swing in sunny California, is the picture of health: tanned, rested, and vigorous. Kennedy exhibits a youthful glow and easy charm seemingly made for TV. Nixon, as critics later quip, has a good face for radio.

dumb LUCK:

And that's exactly how the debates play out in the mind of the American voting public. Substantively a dead heat, radio listeners crown Nixon the debate winner. In stark contrast, the 70 million who watch on TV pronounce Kennedy the victor—and by a wide margin.

after THOUGHTS:

That November, Kennedy wins the election by a nose (a mere 112,000 votes out of 68 million ballots cast). And over 50 percent of all voters report that the four Nixon/Kennedy debates influenced their vote.

More of the Best of the Worst: Ten of the Worst Movie Ideas in History

Bad idea 1: *Glen or Glenda*.

Year: 1953

Auteur: Writer-director-star Ed Wood

Synopsis: Keeping abreast (so to speak) of George Jorgensen's world-rocking sex-change transformation into Christine Jorgensen, first-time film director Wood indulges his inner transvestite by cavorting through this pseudoscientific exploration into gender reassignment while wearing a women's cashmere sweater. Narrated by an aged Béla Lugosi, the film features an inexplicable stampede of bison, S&M fantasies, and the heretofore-unsubstantiated theory that hats cause male pattern baldness.

Review: Film critic Leonard Maltin considers *Glen or Glenda* "possibly the worst movie ever made."

Bad idea 2: *Plan 9 from Outer Space.*
Year: 1959
Auteur: Director Ed Wood (yes, him again)
Synopsis: In this cinematic gem, humans are on course to create a doomsday weapon that just might destroy the universe. So right-minded aliens come to Earth with "Plan 9" to stop them. Spending a few bucks on special effects, Wood utilizes inverted pie tins suspended from clearly visible strings as flying saucers. He then adds snappy dialogue, such as: "Future events such as these will affect you in the future." And clumsily edits in footage of former *Dracula* star Béla Lugosi (shot for an entirely different film) to create a truly absurd, incomprehensible, unintended laugh fest.
Review: Feted by critic Michael Medved with a Golden Turkey Award as the worst movie ever made, the DVD artwork actually proclaims: "Almost starring Béla Lugosi."

Bad idea 3: *The Beast of Yucca Flats.*
Year: 1961
Auteur: Writer-director Coleman Francis
Synopsis: Imagine the horror of a mild-mannered scientist, accidentally exposed to atomic radiation, as he watches himself change into a hideous, murderous monster. Now imagine the horror of watching a movie featuring this scenario shot entirely without sound (with actors filmed facing *away* from the camera so their dialogue could be added later by studio announcers, eschewing the need to lip-synch). Tack on a gratuitous topless scene unrelated to the plot (edited in because the director apparently just sort of likes nude scenes)—plus characters with magically healing gunshot wounds—and you've got the true horror of *The Beast.*

Review: *Leonard Maltin's TV and Movie Guide* calls this "one of the worst films ever made." Another critic deems it possibly "the worst non-porno science-fiction movie ever made." It's also featured on IMDb's bottom 100 movie list.

Bad idea 4: *Eegah.*
Year: 1962
Auteur: Producer-director-writer Nicholas Merriweather
Synopsis: Spotlighting, as its one sheet claims, "the crazed love of a prehistoric giant for a ravishing teenage girl," the film features future James Bond nemesis Jaws (Richard Kiel) as the eponymous caveman. A strange combination of '60s surf film and '50s B-monster flick, *Eegah* showcases the son of the film's financier, Arch Hall Jr., crooning Elvis-style while the tall, hairy beast makes off with his girlfriend. Later, the giant troglodyte eats shaving cream. Appetizing fun for the whole family.
Review: Made for $15,000, *Eegah* earns approximately $3,200 at the box office. It also makes Medved's book *The Fifty Worst Films of All Time.*

Bad idea 5: *The Creeping Terror.*
Year: 1964
Auteur: Producer-director-star Vic Savage
Synopsis: Draped in what appears to be shag carpeting and wearing tennis shoes, large, slug-like aliens slink across the fictitious Angel County, California, countryside looking for—and swallowing whole—a variety of human prey. Slow moving and without arms, the creatures require lots of cooperation from their victims, who, it logically seems, could simply run away rather than allow themselves to be eaten. *The Creeping Terror*

is memorable for its use of bargain-basement special effects, such as stock footage of a rocket launch played in reverse to depict the landing of an alien spacecraft.

Review: TV's *Mystery Science Theater 3000* gives *The Creeping Terror* bad-movie props by lampooning it in 1994.

Bad idea 6: *Santa Claus Conquers the Martians.*
Year: 1964
Auteur: Director Nicholas Webster
Synopsis: Parents on Mars, concerned that their children only get to see Santa Claus on TV transmissions intercepted from Earth, decide to kidnap St. Nick and hold him hostage on the red planet. All manner of interplanetary intrigue culminates when Martian king Kimar's dumb-but-lovable servant Dropo learns the ways of Kringle, eventually earning the right to become Mars's very own version of St. Nick and thereby allowing the real Santa to return home in time for the next Earth Christmas.

Review: Featuring an eight-year-old Pia Zadora, *SCCM* is cited on a ten-worst-film list in *The Book of Lists* and in the 2004 DVD documentary *The 50 Worst Movies Ever Made.*

Bad idea 7: *Ishtar.*
Year: 1987
Auteur: Writer-director Elaine May
Synopsis: Conceived as a modern turn on the classic Bob Hope/Bing Cosby *Road to...* films, *Ishtar* centers on a bumbling singer-songwriter team caught in conflict between the CIA and local guerrillas in Morocco. Plagued by a clunky script, infighting between star Warren Beatty and May, huge cost overruns, scads of negative press, and a dead-on-arrival premier, it remains one of the most expensive comedies ever

made ($55 million). *Ishtar* eventually earns just over $14 million. And May never directs a film again.

Reviews: Nominated for Worst Picture and Worst Screenplay in the 1987 Golden Raspberry Awards—while winning one for Worst Director—*Ishtar* has since become synonymous with "box office flop."

Bad idea 8: *Stop! Or My Mom Will Shoot.*
Year: 1992
Auteur: Director Roger Spottiswoode
Synopsis: Hard-knock cop Joe Bomoski (Sylvester Stallone) has his life turned upside down when his ailing and aged mother (Estelle Getty) comes to stay with him—eventually becoming his pistol-wielding, crime-fighting partner. Yeah, really.
Reviews: Critic Roger Ebert gives the appropriately titled *Stop!* a half-star in his review, calling it "so dimwitted, so utterly lacking in even the smallest morsel of redeeming value, that you stare at the screen in stunned disbelief." Stallone himself later admits it's the worst film he's ever made.

Bad idea 9: *Freddy Got Fingered.*
Year: 2001
Auteur: Writer-director-star Tom Green
Synopsis: In his madcap search for a TV production contract, a slacker cartoonist played by Green engages in such creepily unfunny antics as accusing his father of molesting his younger brother, swinging a newborn baby by its umbilical cord, and playing the piano with sausages. He and actress-wife Drew Barrymore divorce thereafter.
Reviews: CNN's Paul Clinton calls *Freddy* "quite simply

the worst movie ever released by a major studio." Roger Ebert claims the film not only scrapes the bottom of the barrel, but also "doesn't even deserve to be mentioned in the same sentence with barrels." It also appears on Ebert's all-time "most hated" list.

Bad idea 10: *Basic Instinct 2.*
Year: 2001
Auteur: Director Michael Caton-Jones
Synopsis: A masturbation-induced car crash. A sexually explicit rape scene. An orgy. And a therapist manipulated by his patient into committing murder—these are just some of the happy hijinks in the uplifting funfest known as *Basic Instinct 2.* Catherine Trammel (Sharon Stone) is back from her titillating crotch-shot success in *Basic Instinct.* The problem is that no one cares, thanks to the sequel's silly, overwrought, and exploitative plot. The naked truth: *BI2* is made for $70 million (of which Stone reportedly banks $10 million) and earns a mere $3.2 million dollars in its opening weekend.
Reviews: The Razzies give the movie the subtitle "Basically, It Stinks Too." The *New York Post* writes: "At this point, there are inflatable toys that are livelier than Stone, but how can you tell the difference?" On the Rotten Tomatoes website, the clunker is included in their top 100 worst-reviewed movies of the last ten years.

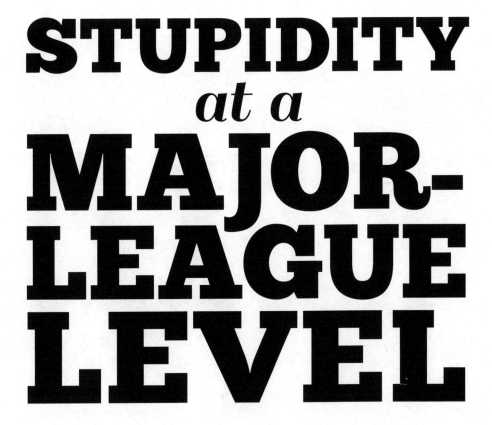

The
BAMBINO'S CURSE
on the BEANTOWN BOMBERS

the
BAD
IDEA:

Sell pitcher Babe Ruth to the New York Yankees.

the genius BEHIND IT:	Harry Frazee, Broadway producer and owner of the Boston Red Sox

the brainstorm STRUCK:	1920

MICHAEL N. SMITH AND ERIC KASUM

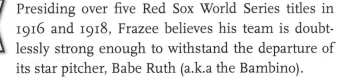

bring on the BLUNDER:

Presiding over five Red Sox World Series titles in 1916 and 1918, Frazee believes his team is doubtlessly strong enough to withstand the departure of its star pitcher, Babe Ruth (a.k.a the Bambino).

Scrounging for cash to finance his Broadway plays, the Sox owner decides to sell Ruth to the Yankees for $100,000 in cash and $300,000 in loans.

from bad TO WORSE:

Frazee can only gape in disbelief as Ruth goes on to single-handedly transform the game, becoming baseball's lifetime home run leader, the most popular athlete of his day, and a charter member of the baseball Hall of Fame in leading the formerly downtrodden Yankees to seven championships in fifteen years.

dumb LUCK:

The Red Sox, on the other hand, endure eight decades of flubs, blunders, and near-misses—each attributed to "The Curse of the Bambino"—on their way to winning zero World Series titles between Ruth's 1920 departure and 2004.

after THOUGHTS:

In its "Greatest North American Athletes of the Twentieth Century," ESPN ranks Ruth as second only to Michael Jordan. Thanks to the power of the curse, the one Red Sox player on the list, Hall of Famer Ted Williams, never won a World Series title.

FOURTH DOWN
and 70 MILLION TO GO

the BAD IDEA: Blend elements of pro football and pro wrestling into a new sports league called the XFL.

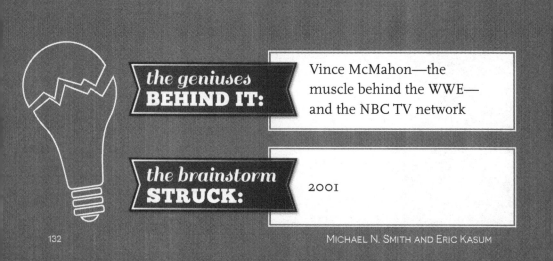

the geniuses BEHIND IT: Vince McMahon—the muscle behind the WWE—and the NBC TV network

the brainstorm STRUCK: 2001

MICHAEL N. SMITH AND ERIC KASUM

bring on the BLUNDER:

Hyped as tough, high-energy, offseason alternatives to the venerable National Football League, XFL games boast blaring rock music, opposing players wrestling at midfield to determine who gets the ball, trash-talking coaches, no penalties for excessive roughness, and lingerie-clad cheerleaders.

Interest piques, then quickly wanes as fans and the media soon sour to the league's phony, pro-wrestling-style machismo, sensationalism, and shoddy play.

from bad TO WORSE:

In week one, XFL games garner respectable TV ratings. But by season's end, a game between the Chicago Enforcers and the New York/New Jersey Hitmen sets a record at the time for the lowest-rated primetime network show in TV history.

dumb LUCK:

All told, the XFL loses $70 million—and suffers a sudden death after a single ten-game season.

after THOUGHTS:

Despite the league's infamous failure, overhead sky cameras, in-game interviews, and helmet microphones are legacies of the XFL still in use today. And the lingerie-clad cheerleaders? They set the stage for the Lingerie Bowl, starting in 2004, where scantily clad women play seven-on-seven tackle football in a pay-per-view TV special held during halftime of the Super Bowl.

The HEAVYWEIGHT CHOMPING-ON of THE WORLD

the BAD IDEA: Bite off a piece of your opponent's ear during a heavyweight boxing title fight.

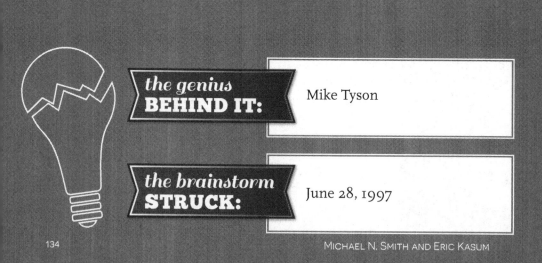

the genius **BEHIND IT:** Mike Tyson

the brainstorm **STRUCK:** June 28, 1997

MICHAEL N. SMITH AND ERIC KASUM

Anger? Hunger for glory? Whatever's motivating former boxing champion Mike Tyson this night, he wants to regain the heavyweight crown so badly he can taste it. Literally.

On the heels of his shocking loss to Evander Holyfield—a 25-to-1 underdog—just eight months before, Tyson is desperate to win back his title. Agitated by what he perceives to be Holyfield's continual, intentional head-butting, Tyson clinches with Holyfield at center ring—and proceeds to bite off part of his ear, forcefully spitting it onto the canvas. Amid the ensuing chaos, Tyson is disqualified, once again losing to Holyfield.

from bad TO WORSE:

An appalled Nevada State Athletic Commission soon revokes Tyson's boxing license and fines him $3 million.

dumb LUCK:

Without the huge boxing paydays he's grown accustomed to, Tyson begins to feel the bite of his free-spending ways. Listing debts of over $27 million—including $4.5 million owed for cars, $140,000 for two Bengal tigers, and a $2 million bathtub—Tyson's finances smack the canvas in bankruptcy court.

after THOUGHTS:

After the fight, boxing fans wonder what might have possessed Tyson to exhibit such bizarre (even for him) behavior in the ring. Yet former Tyson trainer Teddy Atlas had predicted that Iron Mike, fearing he could not beat Holyfield, would do something— "He'll bite Holyfield. He'll butt him. He'll hit him low."—to disqualify himself. Fight fans were all ears.

OUT OF THE PARK? OUT OF THE QUESTION

the BAD IDEA: Refuse to allow the greatest home run hitter of all time to play in the major leagues.

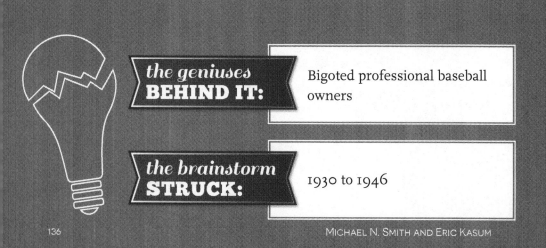

the geniuses BEHIND IT: Bigoted professional baseball owners

the brainstorm STRUCK: 1930 to 1946

MICHAEL N. SMITH AND ERIC KASUM

bring on the BLUNDER:

In any given sports bar on any given night, you'll hear the debate that's raged for generations: Who's the greatest home run hitter of all time?

Some insist it's the legendary Babe Ruth. Others say Hammerin' Hank Aaron. Or a prickly chap named Barry Bonds. But true baseball fans know that the most prolific home run hitter of all time is a man who never played in the major leagues—banned by the game's small-minded stewards because of the color of his skin.

from bad TO WORSE:

Overcoming the tragic death of his wife, who dies giving birth in his rookie season, Josh Gibson, power hitter for the Homestead Grays of the so-called Negro Leagues garners covetous attention from Caucasian baseball scouts across the land.

Crushing towering home run after towering home run, Gibson sees his fame and stature grow. Yet thanks to a "gentleman's agreement" among baseball owners—and despite jacking an estimated 800 homers with an amazing .359 lifetime batting average over seventeen seasons—the African American Gibson never plays in the major leagues.

dumb LUCK:

Diagnosed with a brain tumor in 1943, Josh Gibson later dies of a stroke at the youthful age of thirty-five. Just three months later, baseball owners relent, allowing Jackie Robinson to become the first black player in major league history.

after THOUGHTS:

The majors finally give Gibson his due in 1972, making him the second Negro League player, after Satchel Paige, to be elected to the baseball Hall of Fame.

DOPEY CYCLIST
PEDALS A PACK OF LIES

the BAD IDEA: Cheat to win the biggest bike race in the world, deny it, then confess and accuse other cyclists of cheating as well.

the genius BEHIND IT: Flip-flopping American cyclist Floyd Landis

the brainstorm STRUCK: 2006

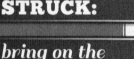

bring on the BLUNDER: Against the wishes of his devout Mennonite father, a young Floyd Landis sneaks out of the house at 2 a.m. each morning to practice his beloved cycling on the frozen hills of Farmersville, Pennsylvania.

Floyd's dogged determination leads him to the U.S. junior national championship in 1993, a spot on the U.S. Postal Service cycling team in 2002, and—despite a painful degenerative hip condition—to a surprise victory in the heralded Tour de France four years later. But immediately, controversy slams on the brakes.

After the race, drug testing shows that Landis's urine contains an unusually high ratio of testosterone. In reaction, he's stripped of his cherished Tour de France victory and banned from the sport.

An outraged Landis vehemently denies the use of any performance-enhancing drugs. His legal team attacks the testing laboratory's procedures and analysis. Desperate for cash, Landis also solicits friends, family, and fans to donate to his legal defense fund. An estimated $1 million is collected.

**dumb
LUCK:**

Following a tumultuous forty-eight-month battle to clear his name and reinstate his Tour de France victory, Landis suddenly, shockingly confesses to the doping charges. What's more, he accuses seven-time-Tour-winner Lance Armstrong and other top riders of doing the same.

Armstrong initially denies Landis's charges, terming him "bitter" after being denied a place on the Armstrong-led Radio Shack racing team in 2010. However, in an ironic twist, Armstrong is stripped of his seven Tour de France titles under a torrent of doping accusations by fellow teammates in 2012—and later admits to doping throughout his career in an interview with Oprah Winfrey.

**after
THOUGHTS:**

Also in 2012, a judge agrees to drop wire-fraud charges against Landis, now out of competitive cycling, in exchange for repaying over $475,000 contributed by supporters to his defense.

A MULTIMILLION-DOLLAR CAREER GOES TO THE DOGS

the genius BEHIND IT: Michael Vick

the brainstorm STRUCK: 2007

bring on the BLUNDER:

Talk about fantasy football: You're the number one pick in the 2001 NFL draft. You make, in 2006, an estimated $26 million. You've been selected to the elite Pro Bowl three times. And the corporate endorsement dollars are rolling in like a green tsunami.

If you're the average pigskin-lovin' American male living this dream life, you might want to throw a megaparty. If you're Michael Vick, you'd rather throw an innocent dog against a wall.

Acting on grand jury testimony alleging that Vick is financing and hosting a high-priced dog fighting ring at his Virginia estate, authorities in July 2007 indict the NFL star on felony counts of animal abuse and gambling.

Prosecutors cite disturbing sworn eyewitness statements claiming that Vick bet as much as $40,000 on a single fight—and that he himself was involved in executing underperforming dogs by hanging, drowning, electrocuting, and "slamming [them] into a brick wall."

**dumb
LUCK:**

After initial denials, Vick pleads guilty and is sentenced to twenty-three months in Leavenworth. Corporate endorsers head for the hills—and Vick's finances head for the pits. Three of his six homes are liquidated. His $300,000-a-month entourage is forced to find succor (or is it a sucker?) elsewhere. Creditors—from banks to angry business partners to his former agents—sue him for millions in damages.

Broke, Vick—by now earning a dollar a day in prison—files for bankruptcy. The nearly fifty dogs found at his Virginia home are relocated to animal shelters and foster care.

**after
THOUGHTS:**

Upon his prison release in 2009, Vick inks a deal with the Philadelphia Eagles. In 2010, he's named the NFL's Comeback Player of the Year and earns his fourth trip to the Pro Bowl. The following year, he signs a six-year, $100 million deal with the Eagles. In 2012 and 2013, injury and poor play relegate him to the bench.

DISCO INFERNO
SINGES *the* WHITE SOX

the BAD IDEA: Disco Demolition Night.

the geniuses BEHIND IT:	Chicago radio DJ Steve Dahl and White Sox executive Mike Veeck
the brainstorm STRUCK:	July 12, 1979

bring on the BLUNDER:

Just your typical day at the ballpark: First, you see a pitcher smoke a fastball down the middle of the plate. Then, you watch a speedy runner burn up the base paths. Finally, you see center field explode in a fireball.

Okay, so it's not exactly your average trip to the old ball game. But that's the whole, record-breaking idea behind "Disco Demolition Night." The brainchild of wildchild Chi-Town radio jock Steve Dahl, DDN promises admission to a White Sox doubleheader for just 98 cents plus an old disco record.

Between games, Dahl collects the unwanted discs, piles them up in the outfield, then uses explosives to blow the vinyl platters to smithereens.

Upon detonation, a crater forms in the outfield. Vinyl shards fly like shrapnel through the air. A fire erupts. Fueled by copious amounts of booze and weed, the rowdy disco-despising crowd then spills onto the field. Thousands more waiting outside the stadium hurtle the turnstiles to join them.

Soon, a full-scale riot is raging, with fans wrecking a batting cage, gouging the infield turf, and burning banners before police rush in to quell the fray. Six people are injured. Nearly forty more are arrested.

dumb
LUCK:

Detroit Tiger manager Sparky Anderson, citing safety concerns, refuses to allow his team onto the field for game two of the doubleheader. And because their home field is now unfit to play on, the White Sox are forced to forfeit the game, marking the last time in history an American League team is dealt an automatic loss.

after
THOUGHTS:

In a later interview, Dahl unrepentantly brags that the event hastened disco's demise. Mike Veeck recedes from baseball, not resurfacing until 1993 as part-owner of a minor league team in St. Paul, Minnesota.

NOT A GUY YOU WANT TO NECK WITH

the
BAD
IDEA:

Date or marry O. J. Simpson, NFL Hall of Fame halfback.

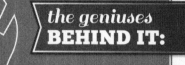

the geniuses
BEHIND IT: Marguerite Simpson, Nicole Simpson, and others

the brainstorm
STRUCK: 1967 to 2008

MICHAEL N. SMITH AND ERIC KASUM

bring on the BLUNDER:

Given O. J. Simpson's combination of looks, charisma, and athletic talent, it's no wonder girls lose their heads (sometimes literally) when the slashing running back is around. But one of the NFL's all-time great rushers is also one of America's all-time worst mates.

It starts with eighteen-year-old Marguerite L. Whitley, the Bay Area babe O. J. weds in 1967. Days before the birth of their third child, Simpson meets eighteen-year-old Nicole Brown and decides to punt away his marriage. Ex-wife Marguerite later sues O. J. for unpaid alimony and child support.

from bad TO WORSE:

It's 1994. Now—second wife Nicole is nearly decapitated outside her Brentwood condo. A criminal jury finds Simpson not guilty of her murder, while a civil jury later finds him liable, with a $33.5 million judgment.

But O. J. keeps scoring. Former model Paula Barbieri dates Simpson after his murder acquittal, but then leaves him because of his "lies and betrayals."

dumb LUCK:

The Juice's most recent squeeze, Christie Prody, is just nineteen years old when she falls under O. J. Svengali's spell. In a *National Enquirer* exclusive, she reveals that Simpson confessed to her that he killed Nicole—and that he's regularly threatened to kill Prody too.

after THOUGHTS:

Simpson is convicted in 2008 on robbery, kidnapping, and weapons charges involving a sports memorabilia dispute. He's now serving time in a Nevada prison, where his next mate is more likely to be named Nick than Nicole.

WAR STRATEGIES that BOMBED

WE QAEDA SORTA ATTACKED *the* WRONG COUNTRY

👎 **the BAD IDEA:** Respond to the 9/11 terrorist attacks by invading Iraq.

the geniuses BEHIND IT: U.S. secretary of defense Donald Rumsfeld, Vice President Dick Cheney, and the neoconservative establishment

the brainstorm STRUCK: March 2003

bring on the BLUNDER: September 11, 2001. Like December 7, 1941, it's a day destined to live in infamy. The United States is attacked by nineteen airline hijackers sponsored by the Afghani-based terrorist group al-Qaeda. The twin towers in New York City fall. Over 2,900 die.

Vowing to serve justice and protect America, the brain trust of the newly elected George W. Bush administration strategizes a military invasion of Afghanistan and...*Iraq?*

MICHAEL N. SMITH AND ERIC KASUM

Connecting al-Qaeda to Iraqi president Saddam Hussein—thereby implicating Hussein in the 9/11 invasion and identifying his "weapons of mass destruction" as a direct threat to U.S. security—Bush pushes the start button on Operation Iraqi Freedom.

Without UN backing, a coalition force comprised primarily of 250,000 American and 45,000 British forces attacks Iraq. In three weeks, Saddam's repressive, larcenous, murderous Ba'athist government is toppled. Landing on the carrier USS *Abraham Lincoln*, President Bush stands in front of a banner declaring, "Mission Accomplished." Only, it wasn't.

dumb
LUCK:

While planning for the war was precise, planning for the aftermath was sorely lacking. With the country's institutions in shambles, widespread looting, arson, and bombings ensue. Too few in number to keep the peace, coalition forces are soon regarded by the locals as occupiers rather than the "conquering heroes" Bush advisors had predicted.

Unaccountable private contractors are brought in to quell the chaos. But the indefinite detention of Iraqi citizens without charges, the alleged torture of prisoners at Abu Ghraib, the war's billion-dollar-a-week price tag, and thousands of casualties gradually turn public opinion against the war—while contributing to the election of antiwar presidential candidate Barack Obama.

after
THOUGHTS:

Ironically, to date, inspectors have found no weapons of mass destruction in Iraq. The intelligence that set the predicate for the war has been seriously challenged. And Hussein's complicity in the 9/11 attack on the United States has been roundly discredited.

A SINGLE TORPEDO SINKS *the* GERMAN SHIP OF STATE

the BAD IDEA:

Attack the British Royal Mail Ship: the *Lusitania*.

the genius BEHIND IT:

German U-boat captain Walther Schwieger

the brainstorm STRUCK:

May 7, 1915

MICHAEL N. SMITH AND ERIC KASUM

bring on the BLUNDER:

"Fire the torpedoes and sink her!" exclaims Captain Schwieger as he finds the *Lusitania* cruising through his U-boat's periscope cross hairs. Members of his crew are aghast. Yes, Britain and Germany are fiercely waging World War I. And, yes, German submarines are under orders to disrupt enemy supply shipments in the North Atlantic. But ruthlessly attack a defenseless passenger ship?

One explosion, then another, tears a gaping hole in the *Lusitania*'s hull, sinking the Cunard liner in a mere eighteen minutes. Over 1,200 civilians die, including scores of wealthy, influential Americans traveling abroad. An outraged world denounces Germany. U.S. president Woodrow Wilson contemplates America's response.

from bad TO WORSE:

German officials pointedly claim that the *Lusitania*, far from innocent, was actually a cleverly disguised military supply ship packed with war matériel. British officials scoff at the assertion, terming the vessel "as helpless as a ferry boat."

dumb LUCK:

"Remember the *Lusitania*" becomes the rallying cry as a heretofore isolationist United States soon plunges into World War I, joining British, French, Russian, and other allied forces to tip the balance of power that eventually capsizes Germany's war effort.

after THOUGHTS:

In 2009, a salvage crew using underwater robotics discovers a massive store of live ammunition—the kind used by the British military in WWI—amid the *Lusitania*'s near-century-old wreckage. The only thing "helpless" about this ship, it turns out, were the unwitting men, women, and children who died the day it sank.

The DOUBLE AGENT WHO DOUBLE-CROSSED DER FÜHRER

the BAD IDEA:

Prepare for the biggest Allied invasion of World War II by positioning your troops in the wrong place.

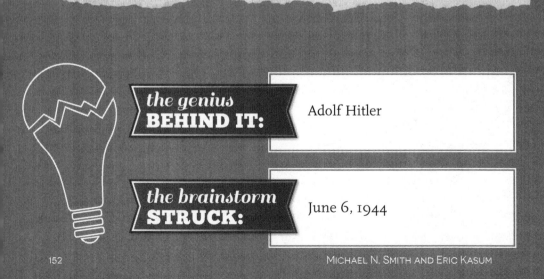

the genius BEHIND IT: Adolf Hitler

the brainstorm STRUCK: June 6, 1944

MICHAEL N. SMITH AND ERIC KASUM

German military intelligence learns that an Allied invasion of Europe is imminent. What they don't know is where or when they will attack.

So Nazi leader Adolf Hitler turns to his most trusted intelligence advisor, Juan Pujol García. But there's one measly little problem with good old Juan: Unbeknownst to Hitler, García is actually a double agent working for the British, code-named "Garbo."

Ever the convincing actor, Garbo advises Hitler with no uncertainty that American general George Patton will storm the beaches of Calais, France.

To validate Garbo's fabrication, the Allies concoct a fake staging zone in England, complete with papier-mâché aircraft. Hitler takes Garbo's apocryphal advice and directs his generals to defend the Calais shores.

Good idea? *Nein.* On June 6, 1944, the real beach-head assault begins miles away in Normandy. Yet so trusted is Garbo's word that Hitler continues to direct his elite Panzer tanks to defend against a sure-to-happen Calais invasion that never happens.

Within a year, Hitler's dream of world domination becomes a nightmare, thanks in no small part to a phony confidant with a phony story and a phony name.

Garbo, his double-agent identity still secret and his Nazi street cred still strong, is awarded Germany's Iron Cross. Simultaneously, he's covertly knighted by the Queen of England—likely the only person in history to be jointly honored as a hero by each opposing side in a war.

INVADE RUSSIA
in the WINTER?
SNOW WAY!

the
BAD
IDEA:

Order a Russian invasion during the chilly season.

the genius **BEHIND IT:** Adolf Hitler (yes, the same mustachioed megalomaniac referenced on the previous page)

the brainstorm **STRUCK:** June 22, 1941

MICHAEL N. SMITH AND ERIC KASUM

France's nineteenth-century wintertime invasion of Russia gave us Tolstoy's *War and Peace*, Tchaikovsky's *1812 Overture*, and Napoleon's worst ass-kicking to date. But evidently, Nazi leader Adolf Hitler doesn't read novels, listen to classical music, or study history. Because he's about to repeat the diminutive French general's monumental strategic blunder.

from bad
TO WORSE:

Emboldened by its blitzkrieging conquests of Poland and France, Hitler's Third Reich now controls much of Europe. The next domino Mr. Goose Step would like to flick over: Russia. And with Operation Barbarossa, he orders his army eastward for the largest military invasion in human history.

Marshaling 4.5 million Axis troops, Hitler's army floods into Russia. Brimming with characteristic hubris, der Führer ignores the imminent, treacherous Russian winter. And he overrules his generals, insisting that his army bypass Moscow in favor of a potentially casualty-intensive, house-to-house foray into Stalingrad.

dumb
LUCK:

The fighting rages for more than six months—and the Stalingrad snow runs red with blood. It soon becomes the most costly battle ever waged. German losses: 750,000 killed, wounded, or missing—and 91,000 captured. Over 900 Nazi aircraft, 4,000 tanks, and 15,000 artillery pieces are lost.

after
THOUGHTS:

Operation Barbarossa and the Battle of Stalingrad humble Hitler's delusion of world domination, break the back of the German army, and drive Stalin's forces into partnership with the soon-to-be-U.S.-led Allies. Like Bonaparte's, Hitler's dream is blown apart.

A MILITARY STRATEGY THAT'S DEAD ON

the geniuses **BEHIND IT:**	Japanese political and military leaders
the brainstorm **STRUCK:**	July 28, 1945
bring on the **BLUNDER:**	American incendiary bombs rain hellfire on Japanese cities. Civilian casualties mount. Homes are reduced to ash. Manufacturing plants collapse into rubble. The economy tumbles as morale wanes. The world is witnessing the final harrowing act of World War II.

American incendiary bombs rain hellfire on Japanese cities. Civilian casualties mount. Homes are reduced to ash. Manufacturing plants collapse into rubble. The economy tumbles as morale wanes. The world is witnessing the final harrowing act of World War II.

But Japanese leaders see things differently. Rising from the smoke and flames of their beaten country, they issue an audacious directive—a directive to the battle-weary Japanese people that defies the obvious and denies the inevitable: "Fight on! Fight to the death!"

MICHAEL N. SMITH AND ERIC KASUM

from bad TO WORSE:

Germany's surrender already in hand, U.S. president Truman and Allied leaders, on July 26, issue the Potsdam Declaration, which outlines the terms of surrender for Japan. It threatens "the complete destruction of the Japanese armed forces and the utter devastation of the Japanese homeland."

Two days later, Prime Minister Kantaro Suzuki states that his government intends to ignore the declaration. At the same time, in the face of incessant, deadly Allied air raids, Emperor Hirohito nonetheless orders his people to battle on—at all costs.

dumb LUCK:

The result is death and destruction of historic proportions: On August 6, an Allied atomic bomb levels Hiroshima. Three days later, a second nuclear explosive obliterates Nagasaki. Over 200,000 are killed. Less than a week hence, Japan surrenders, finally ending the Second World War.

after THOUGHTS:

Japan's resolve to fight to the last is evident in the rise of Kamikaze suicide missions near the conclusion of the conflict. Almost 4,000 Japanese pilots give up their lives by intentionally crashing their aircraft into Allied ships. Historians, studying what inspired Japanese men in the prime of their lives to act in this way, point to a unique mixture of Japan's ancient warrior tradition, societal pressures of the day, economic necessity, and sheer desperation.

YOU BETTER WATCH OUT, YOU BETTER NOT CRY, YOU BETTER READ YOUR MAIL, I'M TELLING YOU WHY: SNEAKY GEORGE IS COMING TO TOWN

the BAD IDEA:

Believe that your enemy wouldn't dream of attacking you on Christmas Day.

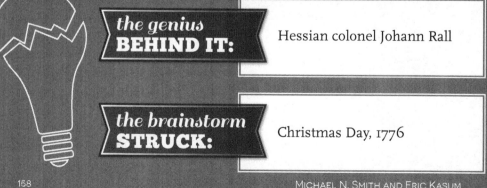

the genius BEHIND IT: Hessian colonel Johann Rall

the brainstorm STRUCK: Christmas Day, 1776

Michael N. Smith and Eric Kasum

bring on the BLUNDER:

The Revolutionary War is on holiday break. On one side of the Delaware River, Hessian troops (in league with the British) open casks of rum and have a "Ho-ho-ho!" lot of fun celebrating Christmas Eve. On the other side, George Washington and his ragtag colonial troops sit quietly in the cold—eager to show the enemy who's naughty or nice.

Enjoying the Yuletide frivolity, Colonel Rall, the Hessian commander, is engrossed in a high-stakes card game when a messenger hands him a note. Rall rails: "Not now! I'll read it later. Can't you see I'm busy?" He snatches the note, carelessly stuffs it into his pocket, and parties on.

from bad TO WORSE:

At first light, General Washington and his men cross the Delaware, descending upon the unsuspecting mercenaries with a fierce sneak attack. The Colonials rout the hungover Hessians in less than an hour. More than 900 prisoners are taken. Colonel Rall himself is critically wounded.

dumb LUCK:

With his last ounce of strength, Rall finally reads the note he had so cavalierly ignored. Written on that bloodied shred of paper is a warning of Washington's impending surprise attack. Regret-stricken, Rall later falls dead.

after THOUGHTS:

By playing his cards wrong, Colonel Rall hands the Colonial Army one of the most important victories in the American war for independence. Without him, you might be sipping tea and munching crumpets as you read this book.

CAESAR'S FIERY BATTLE TACTICS LEAVE HISTORIANS BURNING MAD

the BAD IDEA:

Inadvertently burn down the world's greatest library while torching your own navy.

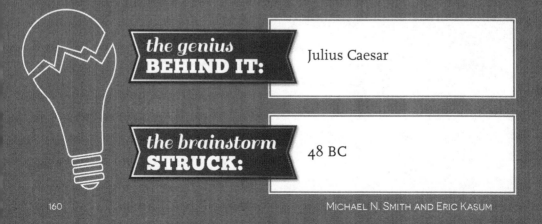

the genius BEHIND IT: Julius Caesar

the brainstorm STRUCK: 48 BC

MICHAEL N. SMITH AND ERIC KASUM

It stands as the greatest repository of knowledge on Earth. The envy of scholars everywhere. People travel months, even years, on foot and on horseback to gaze in wonder at its nearly 500,000 papyrus scrolls—the sum of history, science, language, mathematics, and legend in the ancient world.

This is the magnificent Library of Alexandria, Egypt. But on this tragic night in 48 BC, the library meets a hellish fate. Catching fire, the library and its dry papyrus scrolls combust in moments. Nearly all the scrolls are lost—including, it's said, original books of the Bible, Aesop's Fables, and the first writings of Homer. And behind all the flaming mayhem is the most unlikely of culprits. Although Roman intellectuals and government officials are said to covet the library and its vast volumes, Julius Caesar himself is blamed for sparking the fire.

from bad
TO WORSE:

Caesar—known as a dedicated book-learner who rose to become an impressive legal advocate, orator, and military mind—accidentally sets it ablaze while torching his own ships in Alexandria harbor, a gutsy (or foolhardy) tactic designed to divert his Egyptian opponents during a battle contesting the reign of Cleopatra.

dumb
LUCK:

Roman reinforcements eventually carry Caesar to victory. But he's lambasted for the next 2,000 years for destroying perhaps the greatest compendium of knowledge the world had ever—or has ever—seen.

after
THOUGHTS:

Imagine the wisdom future generations might have gained had these invaluable writings been preserved.

America's
BEST GENERAL
GETS A SLAP IN THE FACE

the BAD IDEA:

Teach a soldier self-respect by slapping him in the face.

the genius **BEHIND IT:**

U.S. Army general George S. Patton

the brainstorm **STRUCK:**

August 3, 1943

MICHAEL N. SMITH AND ERIC KASUM

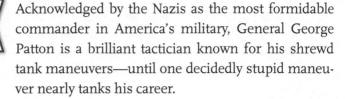

bring on the BLUNDER:

Acknowledged by the Nazis as the most formidable commander in America's military, General George Patton is a brilliant tactician known for his shrewd tank maneuvers—until one decidedly stupid maneuver nearly tanks his career.

While visiting the wounded, Patton comes upon Private Charles Kuhl resting on the edge of his hospital bed. The seemingly fit Kuhl confesses to Patton that he can no longer take the harrowing tension of the front lines. "It's my nerves..." he pleads.

from bad TO WORSE:

Seething with rage, the irate general slaps the young man across the face, calling him a coward and ordering him back into battle.

dumb LUCK:

Within days, Supreme Allied Commander Dwight Eisenhower slaps Patton down—pointing out that Kuhl had malaria at the time of the slapping incident—and demands that the general apologize to his men for "abuse of the sick."

Following the revelation of Patton's free-swinging outbursts, the nation grows incensed. As public pressure builds, Eisenhower relieves Patton of his Seventh Army command. And rather than lead the Allied invasion of Europe, as Nazi leaders fear, he's merely used as a decoy.

after THOUGHTS:

A humbled Patton returns to march the Third Army to victory in 1944's Battle of the Bulge. Ironically, having survived the hazards of countless such battles, he's injured in a car accident on a German street in December 1945—and dies twelve days later.

More of the Best of the Worst: Fashion Frock-Ups

Pick Your Favorite Worst Ideas for Under-, Outer-, Foot-, and Headwear

The bad idea: Leisure suits.
The brainstorm struck: 1970s
We can see your blunderwear: Even Travolta looks revolting in this polyester disaster.

The bad idea: The corset.
The brainstorm struck: Sixteenth century
We can see your blunderwear: Cinch it up and prepare to pass out.

The bad idea: Platform shoes.
The brainstorm struck: 1970s
We can see your blunderwear: The new height of style—a new low in taste. Free sprained ankle with every pair.

The bad idea: Trucker hats.
The brainstorm struck: 1970s, revived in the 2000s
We can see your blunderwear: Begs the question, who the truck looks good in this retro headwear?

The bad idea: Wooden shoes.
The brainstorm struck: 1700s
We can see your blunderwear: A stiff, hard building material to walk around in. What's next, stainless-steel chinos?

The bad idea: The toupee.
The brainstorm struck: 3100 BC
We can see your blunderwear: Ear-to-ear carpeting for the folliclely challenged man is often little more than a bald-faced lie.

The bad idea: Clip-on ties.
The brainstorm struck: 1960s
We can see your blunderwear: Why hide your laziness when you can hang it from your neck for all the world to see?

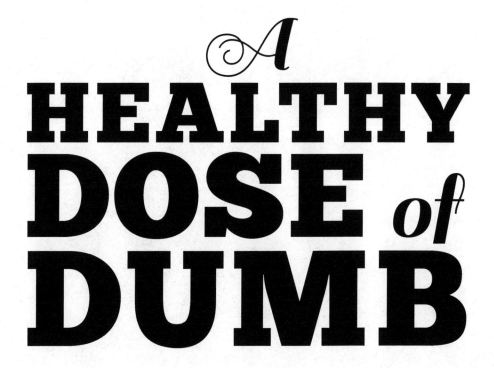

A HEALTHY DOSE of DUMB

HATS OFF *to the* WORLD'S MADDEST PROFESSION

the BAD IDEA:

Use poisonous mercury to fashion and clean felt hats.

the geniuses BEHIND IT:	British "hatters" or hatmakers
the brainstorm STRUCK:	Around 1830

MICHAEL N. SMITH AND ERIC KASUM

bring on the BLUNDER:

In the race to create fashion-forward, Euro-hip menswear, nineteenth-century hatmakers aren't using their heads.

Selecting the finest Turkish camel hair with which to produce hat felt, they discover that soaking the fibers in camel urine greatly enhances quality and manufacturing efficiency. Years later, more abundant and available human urine is used in its place. (Gross yet effective.)

from bad TO WORSE:

Curiously, over time, hatmakers find that urine from humans being treated for syphilis helps produce the best felt of all, thanks to a medication containing mercury. By the mid-1800s, human urine gives way to mercury nitrate, a chemical solution that becomes a prime ingredient in hat manufacturing and care.

dumb LUCK:

But just as mercury makes for beautiful hats, it does ugly things to the human body and mind—giving rise to angry psychotic reactions, irritable dementia, delirium, hallucinations, tremors, and suicidal thoughts. It also gives currency to the phrase "mad as a hatter," in reference to the bizarre behavior and physical abnormalities brought on by hatmakers' prolonged exposure to the powerful neurotoxin.

after THOUGHTS:

In 1941, the U.S. Public Health Service deems mercury poisonous and bans its use in hat manufacturing. Today, the nickname "Mad Hatter" is a quaint throwback to the *Alice in Wonderland* era.

HELP YOURSELF to a STEAMING CUP of INFLUENZA

the BAD IDEA:

Attempt to stop the greatest flu pandemic in history by using heated cups.

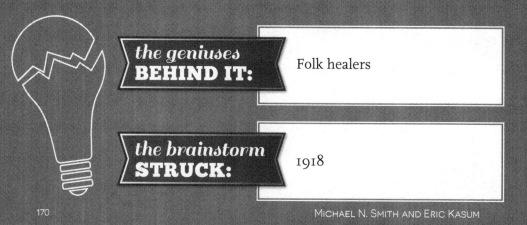

the geniuses BEHIND IT:	Folk healers
the brainstorm STRUCK:	1918

MICHAEL N. SMITH AND ERIC KASUM

Less than a century ago, many of the world's finest medical practitioners contend that diseases are caused by imbalances in the body's "humors"—alleged to be comprised of blood, yellow bile, black bile, and phlegm.

Perhaps more alarmingly, in the absence of licensing, almost anyone can claim to be a "doctor"—from folk healers to your goofy next-door neighbor Fred.

So it should come as no surprise, in the face of the dreaded Spanish influenza pandemic of 1918, that the world is ill prepared to fight its symptoms or find a cure.

from bad
TO WORSE:

As the flu coughs, sneezes, and wheezes its way around the globe, an estimated 675,000 Americans catch it and die. Panic rages. Traditional medical treatments, such as bed rest and isolation, are failing to quell the burgeoning contagion.

dumb
LUCK:

Into this desperate breach comes "cupping," an age-old practice that involves placing a small, heated glass cup on the patient's back to draw out the sickness.

What does cupping do? Well, it leaves round marks, burns, and/or bruises on the skin. What it *doesn't* do is cure the flu. As a result of this and other well-intentioned—but woefully inadequate—medical care, between 30 and 50 million perish worldwide before the Spanish flu runs its course in 1922.

after
THOUGHTS:

Today, we know that simple practices, such as hand washing and covering our mouths when coughing or sneezing, can greatly inhibit the passage of flu viruses.

A
DENTAL CARE PRODUCT
that could
ROT YOUR TEETH

 **the**
BAD
IDEA:
Invent a thick, sugary, cocaine-laced syrup and market it as a health care product.

THE BAD IDEA #2: Sell your rights to what will become the most profitable product of all time.

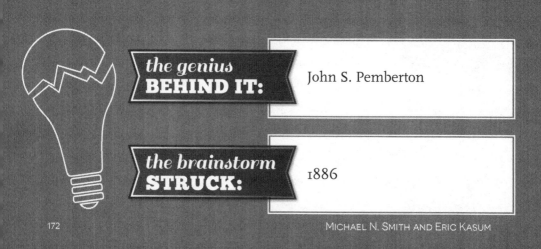

the genius
BEHIND IT: John S. Pemberton

the brainstorm
STRUCK: 1886

MICHAEL N. SMITH AND ERIC KASUM

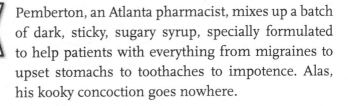

bring on the BLUNDER:

Pemberton, an Atlanta pharmacist, mixes up a batch of dark, sticky, sugary syrup, specially formulated to help patients with everything from migraines to upset stomachs to toothaches to impotence. Alas, his kooky concoction goes nowhere.

from bad TO WORSE:

Then, one fortuitous day, a soda jerk at nearby Jacob's Pharmacy accidentally adds carbonated water to a cup of Pemberton's thick syrup. His mistake tastes so good that customers begin to request it. The bubbly new brew soon finds a loyal following.

dumb LUCK:

Frustrated by the failure of his syrup as a multi-malady remedy—and dismissive of its nonmedicinal possibilities—Pemberton sells the rights to his product recipe to another local pharmacist, Asa Griggs Candler, who seizes on its potential as a "fun drink."

Result: Pemberton and his family members never receive a penny of the megaprofits of what goes on to become the biggest soft drink on Earth: Coca-Cola.

after THOUGHTS:

Today, Coke is the top-selling product in the history of the world, available in more than two hundred countries, with sales of more than $20 million a day. It bestows no known health benefit. (And, it should be noted, no longer contains cocaine.)

LINCOLN'S MERCURY DEALERS
NEARLY DRIVE
THE PRESIDENT CRAZY

the BAD IDEA:

Use a toxic metal to cure depression.

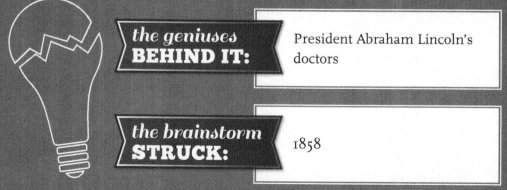

the geniuses **BEHIND IT:** President Abraham Lincoln's doctors

the brainstorm **STRUCK:** 1858

MICHAEL N. SMITH AND ERIC KASUM

bring on the BLUNDER:

With a daunting presidential run ahead of him—and with at least two mental breakdowns behind him—perhaps the greatest leader America has ever seen regularly contemplates death. Desperate for relief, a tall, gawky, insecure Abraham Lincoln seeks treatment for what today might be termed "clinical depression."

But almost immediately after said treatments, Lincoln's typically reserved demeanor explodes into "uncharacteristic fits of rage." His doctors are puzzled.

from bad TO WORSE:

A 2001 study by medical historian Norbert Hirschhorn, MD, might hold the answer. Lincoln's extreme mood swings, he reveals, are caused by a little pill commonly prescribed for melancholia in the 1800s called "blue mass."

Physicians of the day believe the high doses of mercury contained in the pills flush the liver and brain of irritants that cause depression. The treatment regime, in Lincoln's case, totally backfires.

dumb LUCK:

His depression worsens. Throughout 1859, Lincoln suffers violent anger, memory loss, and tremors—further symptoms of metal poisoning. Yet despite his intense personal suffering, he soldiers on, running for—and winning—the presidential race the following year.

after THOUGHTS:

Fortunately, when a nation gripped in Civil War needs steady leadership most, Lincoln, anxious to try anything to relieve his darkening mental state, decides to stop taking blue mass. And having done so, he's able to bravely keep the American house undivided through its most divisive era.

The HIPPOCRATIC CURE
ONLY DRACULA COULD LOVE

the
**BAD
IDEA:** Bloodletting.

the geniuses
BEHIND IT:

Ancient Mesopotamian, Egyptian, Greek, Mayan, and Aztec medicine men

the brainstorm
STRUCK:

BCS (Before Common Sense)

bring on the
BLUNDER:

It's the age of Hippocrates. You're a middle-aged Greek man feeling run down. Fortunately, your barber (yes, the same guy who trims your coif) has the cure: He hangs you upside down while slicing open an artery to let your blood drain out.

There, feel better now? No? Well, you're not alone. From the first bud of civilization, man has embarked upon the decidedly uncivilized practice of bloodletting—all without any scientific evidence that it helps make a sick patient healthy. And with plenty of evidence that it helps make a sick patient dead.

MICHAEL N. SMITH AND ERIC KASUM

It all starts with that little monthly "treat" for women known as menstruation. Hippocrates—he of "First Do No Harm" fame—theorizes that menstrual bleeding purges a woman of bad "humors," the body's blood, phlegm, black bile, and yellow bile that doctors of the day believe regulate health. In order to balance the body's humors, the theory states, excess blood must be purged.

While bloodletting is commonly recommended by physicians through the next twenty-plus centuries, it's often performed at the neighborhood barbershop—largely by untrained (and unsanitary) men who, with a Sweeney Todd–like abundance of straight razors, see little difference between cutting your hair and cutting your veins.

dumb LUCK:

By the mid-1800s, the barber-ic practice of bloodletting is thankfully discredited by leading medical professionals. Today, the practice has been largely abandoned, except in the treatment of a narrow array of blood ailments, such as hemochromatosis and polycythemia, and only under the strict supervision of a phlebotomist to assure its effectiveness.

after THOUGHTS:

Legend has it that the traditional red-and-white-striped barber pole, still seen today, is an outgrowth of the barber-as-surgeon era. The red is said to represent blood being drawn, while the white signifies the tourniquet applied to eventually stop the patient's bleeding.

IGNORANCE
is DR. BLISS

👎 the
BAD
IDEA:

Remove an assassin's bullet from President James A. Garfield's abdomen—with extreme prejudice.

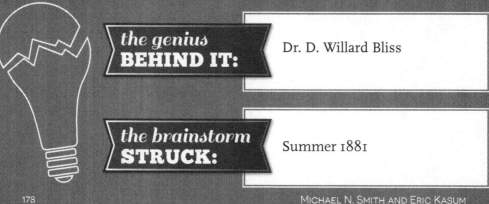

| *the genius* **BEHIND IT:** | Dr. D. Willard Bliss |

| *the brainstorm* **STRUCK:** | Summer 1881 |

MICHAEL N. SMITH AND ERIC KASUM

History tells us that President Garfield—who believed that assassination could not be prevented and "is best not worried about"—is shot and killed in a Washington railroad station by an irate diplomat-wannabe named Charles J. Guiteau.

The part about Guiteau shooting Garfield is unquestionably true. But the part about him killing the president is dead wrong.

**from bad
TO WORSE:**

A befuddled team of doctors led by D. Willard Bliss attends to the wounded head of state. Frantically searching for the would-be assassin's bullet, Willard hastily bores an exploratory passageway into Garfield's abdomen—but finds nothing.

He later shoves an unwashed finger into the opening, triggering a raging infection. Another physician goes knuckles-deep into the president's gut—and inadvertently injures his liver. Over the next two months, more than a dozen medical "experts" do their part to turn a small bullet hole into a gaping, oozing, fetid, twenty-inch canal.

**dumb
LUCK:**

Eighty excruciating days after the shooting, the agonized Garfield mercifully dies. Ironically, an autopsy shows that the elusive bullet is lodged safely away from critical organs or blood vessels. The president, examiners conclude, likely would have survived if his doctors had simply followed the Hippocratic oath: First do no harm.

**after
THOUGHTS:**

At trial, Guiteau's defense hinges on the fact that he, in fact, did not kill the president. No matter. He's promptly convicted and hanged for murder.

The
DENTAL AMALGAM
THAT MIGHT HAVE YOU FEELING
DOWN *in the* MOUTH

the
BAD
IDEA:

Fill teeth with
toxic mercury.

the genius
BEHIND IT:

G. V. Black, a Chicago dentist

the brainstorm
STRUCK:

1895

bring on the BLUNDER:

Known to be more poisonous than arsenic, mercury would seem to be low on the list of substances you might want to pop into your mouth. Nevertheless, mercury has been a cornerstone of dentistry for over one hundred years.

from bad TO WORSE:

Championed by Dr. Black as a pliable amalgam for filling decayed teeth, silver fillings soon become the gold standard for restorative dentistry. But sink your teeth into this: Such fillings are only about 25 percent silver. The rest? Mostly mercury.

Nonetheless, silver/mercury fillings are approved for use without ever being tested for safety by the Food and Drug Administration—and, yes, with the full support of the powerful American Dental Association.

dumb LUCK:

In 1990, a *60 Minutes* exposé demonstrates that mercury vapor levels in the mouth of at least one patient with traditional dental fillings is three times higher than the U.S. government allows in workplace environments.

Today, medical schools are looking into the relationship between oral mercury vapor and a variety of diseases: Alzheimer's, arthritis, colitis, and others. Yet the substance remains in the mouths of millions of Americans to this day.

after THOUGHTS:

Canada, Sweden, and Britain today recommend against mercury fillings for pregnant women and children. Scientists for the U.S. Environmental Protection Agency later find that one out of eight American women of childbearing age already has so much mercury in her body that she's at risk of having a brain-damaged baby.

BALLOON BOY FLOATS
a STORY FULL *of* HOT AIR

the BAD IDEA: In an airheaded attempt to gain fame, report that your young son is helplessly floating thousands of feet overhead in a homemade helium balloon.

the genius BEHIND IT: Fame-chaser Richard Heene

the brainstorm STRUCK: October 15, 2009

bring on the BLUNDER: National Guard choppers race to the scene in breakneck aerial pursuit. Local Fort Collins, Colorado, police give frenzied chase on the ground below. The Denver airport is hurriedly closed. All while the eyes of a nation are riveted to the strange, saucer-shaped object floating aimlessly overhead.

The UFO 7,000 feet aloft is his own handmade helium balloon, a distraught Richard Heene tells authorities. And inside it, his unwitting six-year-old son, Falcon, lies precariously trapped.

Having drifted more than fifty miles in two hours, the gaseous craft finally, gradually falls to earth. But among the wreckage, the boy is nowhere to be found. Did he plummet from the balloon before it crashed? A frantic search team scours the Colorado countryside for clues.

Sympathy soon turns to suspicion when it's revealed that Heene reported the emergency to a Denver TV station before calling 911. But his Balloon Boy story springs an even bigger leak when he announces, later that day, that Falcon has been found: Never airborne, he'd been hiding in the family garage all along.

But the real "gotcha!" moment occurs that same evening, as the Heene family appears on *Larry King Live*. During the interview, Falcon is asked why he hid out in the garage. Turning to his father, he states: "You said we did this for the show." The entire escapade, Heene soon admits, has been a bizarrely elaborate publicity stunt aimed at garnering him a starring role in his own TV program.

Three days later, the wannabe actor—twice featured on the reality show *Wife Swap* and unsuccessful in attempts to sell his original TV show premise called *Science Detectives*—is arrested on felony charges.

Pleading guilty, Heene is sentenced to ninety days in jail, plus home detention, four years' probation, one hundred hours of community service, and $36,000 in restitution. He and his wife are also banned from accepting any profits stemming from the balloon boy fiasco.

INDIA'S ROLL
of the DICE COMES UP *an* UNLUCKY "SEVIN"

the
**BAD
IDEA:** Operate a chemical plant in a heavily populated area.

the geniuses BEHIND IT: Union Carbide Corporation and the government of India

the brainstorm STRUCK: Late 1970s

bring on the BLUNDER: Long before India becomes the outsourcing darling of Western capitalists, the Indian government of the 1970s slaughters plenty of sacred cows (not to mention its own citizens) in a feverish quest to lure foreign investment.

Say you'd like to ignore the rather obvious hazards inherent in placing a factory that produces the toxic pesticide Sevin in a densely populated city, such as Bhopal. Ignore away, Professor Punjab! In fact, India's governmental mahatmas will actually become your partner in such a venture, as they do with America's Union Carbide Corporation.

MICHAEL N. SMITH AND ERIC KASUM

But the popularity of Sevin deep-sixes soon thereafter. So Union Carbide—with heavily invested government regulators looking the other way—shifts to the manufacturing of more complex, more volatile chemical elements at the same factory.

On December 3, 1984, over forty tons of methyl isocyanate gas leaks from the plant into the Bhopal night. At least 3,800 people die instantly. The company maintains that all safety procedures had been followed, preferring to blame the catastrophe on sabotage by an unnamed employee.

Despite its protestations of innocence, Union Carbide is soon swept up in a deluge of lawsuits—yet wins the right to have the cases heard in Indian rather than U.S. courts. And in an agreement with the Supreme Court of India, the chemical giant eventually agrees to pay $470 million in damages to the victims.

While it's the largest award of its kind in Indian history, $470 million is a fraction of what the victims might have received in an American courtroom. Regardless, as a study later states, the catastrophe's financial and human toll could have been mitigated had the plant been located in an area zoned for hazardous materials—and if government inspectors had done their jobs.

Taking its place as the worst industrial accident ever, the Bhopal toxic gas leak, over time, kills an estimated 15,000 people. In 2011, five victims' rights groups petition for payment of an additional $8.1 billion in compensation. Dow Chemical, now the owner of Union Carbide, refuses, stating that the case has already been settled.

EIGHT
is more than
ENOUGH

the BAD IDEA: Decide as an unemployed single mother of six to undergo risky fertility treatments in order to birth octuplets.

the genius BEHIND IT: Nadya Suleman

the brainstorm STRUCK: 2008

bring on the BLUNDER: Nadya Suleman likes kids. No, seriously, with six already, she *really* likes kids. And the thirty-three-year-old mother would really, really, really, really, really, really, really, really like to have eight more—immediately!

So under the guidance of her doctor, Suleman brushes aside concerns over her history of severe postpartum depression and opts to take the controversial and often dangerous step of having six embryos implanted in her womb at the same time.

Historically, on January 26, 2009, she gives birth to eight babies (two embryos had split into twins)—only the second live set of octuplets ever born in the United States. At the same moment, in a worldwide media explosion, the Octomom is born.

Intrigued by the fact that Suleman is divorced, unemployed, and already has a gaggle of children, the media shine a light on every tidbit of her eccentric life. The public's mood quickly sours. While subsisting on family charity and government support with no visible source of income, she's labeled "irresponsible" and "unfit" to care for fourteen children. Her property is vandalized. Death threats ensue. There's even talk that Suleman might lose custody of all fourteen kids.

**dumb
LUCK:**

Not surprisingly, reality TV comes calling. An Octomom TV show in Great Britain gains momentum, then fizzles amid growing public revulsion. Her mother terms Suleman "overwhelmed" attempting to care for her legion of offspring. And the financer of her small, four-bedroom home in La Habra, California, threatens her with eviction for nonpayment.

**after
THOUGHTS:**

"To help pay the rent," Suleman stars in an X-rated video for Wicked Entertainment in 2012. She also appears at a Florida strip club, taking the stage as a lollipop-licking schoolgirl. Later, in an effort to avoid home foreclosure, she auctions off a fun-filled "date with Octomom" on WhatsYourPrice.com. The opening bid: $500. And in 2014, Los Angeles County charges her with welfare fraud.

Y2K *is* A-OK

the **BAD IDEA:** Create a major hubbub around the little theory of an impending "Millennium Bug."

the geniuses **BEHIND IT:** Tech authors Jerome T. and Marilyn J. Murray

the brainstorm **STRUCK:** 1984

MICHAEL N. SMITH AND ERIC KASUM

bring on the BLUNDER:

In the early days of computerization, software is commonly programmed using the last two digits of a given year to indicate the date. So, according to the Murrays, when December 31, 1999 (12/31/99) turns into January 1, 2000 (1/1/00), computers will incorrectly operate as if the new date is January 1, 1900 (also 1/1/00).

Dire consequences are predicted: Airplanes will fall from the sky. Our defensive missiles will be un-launchable. Broadcast communication will cease. The financial system will collapse.

from bad TO WORSE:

In preparation for this dreaded digital "Armageddon," governments, businesses, and individuals spend over $300 billion to fix or replace aging software in hopes of protecting their computers from the so-called "Millennium Bug." But many others, unpersuaded by the apocalyptic Y2K predictions, take no precautions.

dumb LUCK:

When the clock strikes midnight on December 31, 1999, something remarkable happens: nothing. Those who've spent zilch preparing for the big bad bug have no more computer problems than those who spent millions.

The *Wall Street Journal* later calls the Y2K software scare the equivalent of "an end-of-the-world cult" and "the hoax of the twentieth century."

after THOUGHTS:

In the wake of the Y2K noncalamity, the digital data backup industry rises to new heights—as does public skepticism about scientific predictions, such as the more recent backlash against global warming theories.

THE LONDON
BIG MAC SMACKDOWN

the
BAD
IDEA:

Recommend that your client, the world's largest restaurant chain, sue a postman and a gardener for insulting your burgers.

the geniuses
BEHIND IT:

McDonald's McLegal Team

the brainstorm
STRUCK:

1985

bring on the
BLUNDER:

Long before Morgan Spurlock supersizes our awareness of America's unhealthy obsession with fast food, environmental activists David Morris and Helen Steel camp under London-area golden arches to hand out their pamphlet titled *What's Wrong with McDonald's? Everything They Don't Want You to Know.*

McDonald's burger brass (possibly led by an incensed Mayor McCheese) flips its collective bun lid.

Taking advantage of strict British libel laws, the company, poised with a team of attorneys beefier than a triple Quarter Pounder, sues the financially challenged postman and gardener.

For the next five years, representing themselves, Morris and Steel play courtroom Davids to McDonald's Goliath—rising to the status of working-class heroes. Meanwhile, McDonald's public image tumbles.

dumb
LUCK:

As the sesame seeds settle, concluding the longest-running court action in English history, the sitting judge rules that Morris and Steel's claims, as outlined in their pamphlet, are essentially *true*: that McDonald's "exploits children" with its advertising; is "culpably responsible" for cruelty to animals; is "antipathetic" to unionization; and pays its workers low wages. He then declares the two innocent on all but one count of libel, suspends their sentence, and imposes a fine of 40,000 pounds (just over $60,000 today)—which the pamphleteering pair never pay.

after
THOUGHTS:

Happier than a Happy Meal, Morris and Steel there-after file a countersuit with the European Court of Human Rights. As the court finds in the couple's favor, free speech champions everywhere declare: "I'm lovin' it." Morris and Steel document their unappetizing legal tussle with McDonald's in a 2005 film titled *McLibel*.

Cattlemen's
BEEF WITH OPRAH
NEEDS MORE COWBELL

the BAD IDEA: Pick a fight with media goddess Oprah Winfrey.

the geniuses BEHIND IT: Texas cattle producers

the brainstorm STRUCK: 1996

bring on the BLUNDER: During a hard-charging, hoof-stamping talk show debate over the cattle industry's cannibalistic practice of feeding cow meat to cows—and its possible role in the spread of mad cow disease—host Oprah Winfrey declares: "It has just stopped me cold from eating another burger!"

A group of Texas cowboys ropes Winfrey into court, claiming that her "false defamation of perishable food" (which, amazingly, is against Texas law) has sent their cattle prices tumbling, costing the state's beef industry $12 million in lost sales.

from bad TO WORSE:

America's most well-known and well-spoken billionaire, Oprah is ready and able to bust these bronco bullies. Reacting to claims by cattle industry attorneys that the beloved talk show host "acted as a cheerleader and created a lynch mob mentality" in a biased vendetta against beef eating, Winfrey takes the bull by the horns.

Moving her show to Amarillo, site of the trial, Oprah wages battle inside and outside the courtroom. She books Texas celebrities to appear on her Lone Star–studded show. Nonstop media coverage encourages local residents to picket the courtroom in Winfrey's defense. In Sante Fe, New Mexico, Oprah fans stage a protest, stomping on hamburgers to demonstrate their solidarity.

dumb LUCK:

In the end, the cattle industry's case rings about as true as a broken cowbell. And on February 26, 1998, Oprah is acquitted on all charges. Teary eyed, she shouts to a gathering of supporters: "Free speech not only lives, it rocks!"—adding, tongue-in-cheek, "(But) I'm still off hamburgers."

after THOUGHTS:

Thanks in part to this case, the grotesque practice of feeding cow parts to cattle is against the law today. Nevertheless, it remains legal in pig and chicken farming.

BERNIE MADE-OFF WITH THEIR MONEY

the BAD IDEA: Trust flimflam financier Bernie Madoff with your life savings.

the geniuses BEHIND IT: Thousands of individual and institutional investors worldwide

the brainstorm STRUCK: 1991

bring on the BLUNDER: An erstwhile sprinkler repairman, Bernard L. Madoff is the embodiment of the American dream, parlaying a paltry $5,000 initial investment in his own securities firm in 1960 into a nearly $1 billion dollar personal fortune by 2008.

Shockingly, his American dream becomes a nightmare for thousands of investors who trust his sage advice and reputation for delivering extraordinarily high rates of return. Because Madoff is not, in fact, "the biggest market-maker on NASDAQ." He is, more accurately, one big, fat fraud.

On a December evening in 2008, Madoff admits to his sons, both senior partners in his firm, that the company is struggling to meet nearly $7 billion in payouts requested by investors hard hit by the staggering U.S. economy. He further confesses that, for the past seventeen years, he's been running not an investment firm but rather a Ponzi scheme—an investment fraud that involves the payment of purported returns to existing investors from funds contributed by new investors.

In truth, Madoff divulges, the $65 billion his firm has collected from trusting, well-intentioned individuals, charities, and foundations has largely gone into perpetuating the ruse—and into Madoff's own pocket.

dumb
LUCK:

Sons Mark and Andrew report Dad to the authorities, leading to his arrest. With charges spanning securities fraud, money laundering, perjury, and falsifying SEC filings, the elder Madoff pleads guilty. The sentencing judge hands him a merciless 150 years in prison plus $170 billion in restitution.

after
THOUGHTS:

Targeting the Jewish community, Madoff (himself a Jew) ensnares Yeshiva University, the Women's Zionist Organization of America, Steven Spielberg's Wunderkinder Foundation, plus a number of Jewish federations and hospitals. Some are forced to cease operations. Baseball great Sandy Koufax, talk show host Larry King, and scores of banks, investment houses, corporations, schools, and charities around the world fall for Madoff's scheme. An investigation results in reprimands for seven employees of the Securities and Exchange Commission, but no one is fired.

BREAK GLASS *and* GET THIRTY YEARS *of* BAD LUCK

the BAD IDEA:

Financial industry deregulation.

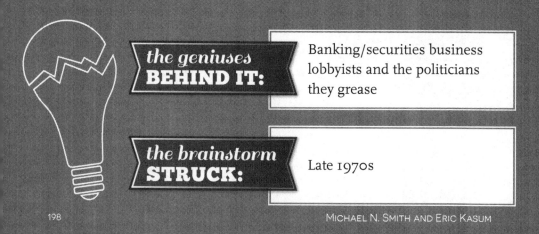

the geniuses **BEHIND IT:**

Banking/securities business lobbyists and the politicians they grease

the brainstorm **STRUCK:**

Late 1970s

MICHAEL N. SMITH AND ERIC KASUM

bring on the BLUNDER:

A study in contrasts: When the Great Depression of the 1920s strikes, the experts argue that America needs financial regulation. Result: the market-calming Glass-Steagall Act of 1933, which establishes federal deposit insurance.

But when the great recession of the late 1970s strikes, the experts argue that America needs financial *deregulation*. Result: the most expensive series of booms, busts, and bailouts our country has ever seen.

from bad TO WORSE:

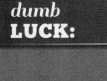

It all starts in 1978. The Supreme Court paves the way for the elimination of bank usury ceilings. Four years later, savings and loans gain the power—yet not the expertise—to offer high-interest, investment-style accounts.

As a consequence, nearly 750 of the nation's thrift institutions fail, costing American taxpayers $87.9 billion.

dumb LUCK:

In 1999, Glass-Steagall is repealed. One year later, famously incomprehensible "credit default swaps" are deregulated. Soon, mortgage lending restrictions are eased—allowing almost anyone to qualify.

Fueled by shaky mortgages, a housing bubble grows. When home values precipitously drop in 2007, fore-closures skyrocket. And the Worldwide Recession of 2008 is born.

after THOUGHTS:

In reaction to the largest economic downturn since the Great Depression, U.S. banks are handed a $700 billion bailout. In the span of three decades, financial deregulation, sold by its proponents as adding value to consumers, has cost Americans nearly $800 billion.

More of the Best of the Worst: What the Flock Were They Thinking?

Straight, Not-So-Straight, and Crooked Preachers

The preacher: Aimee Semple McPherson

The bad idea: "The Fake-Death Radio Shack Up."

Let us pray: One of the leading evangelists and radio personalities of the 1920s and 1930s, McPherson, founder of the Foursquare Church, is thought to have drowned while swimming at Venice Beach, California. One month later, she emerges in the Mexican desert, claiming to have been drugged, kidnapped, and held captive. Meanwhile, eyewitnesses report having spied her sharing a love shack in Carmel, California, with a married radio engineer.

The end cometh: A grand jury finds inconclusive evidence to charge McPherson with faking her own death and kidnapping. She dies from an accidental overdose of barbiturates in 1944.

The preachers: Jim and Tammy Faye Bakker

The bad idea: "The Disneyland-for-Jesus-Freaks Fraud."

Let us pray: Bible school sweethearts who soar to televangelist stardom on the wings of the Christian Broadcasting Network, the endlessly perky Bakker pair cofound the Praise the Lord Network—with 13 million viewers on 1,200 cable systems—and Heritage USA, a religious theme park in North Carolina.

But in 1987, their partnership becomes a roller coaster into hell, as Jim is exposed for having a onetime fling with Long Island church secretary Jessica Hahn—complete with subsequent hush money payments—and for defrauding over 150,000 contributors to his ministry.

The end cometh: The Bakkers resign from PTL, serve prison time, and divorce while in the hoosegow. In 2006, Jim starts a Christian TV show with his second wife. In 2007, Tammy dies of cancer.

The preacher: Jimmy Swaggart

The bad idea: "The Big Easy Sleazy."

Let us pray: At eight, he speaks in tongues at Pentecostal revival meetings. As a teenage evangelist, he rails against the evils of Satan and sings in local band shows with cousins Jerry Lee Lewis and Mickey Gilley. In his forties, he lords over a ministry with its own 195-country TV network. And by age fifty-three, his dalliance with a New Orleans prostitute brings his whole magical, musical Mardi Gras to a halt.

Refusing a disciplinary suspension by the Assemblies of God church, Swaggart is stripped of his leadership position. And after a tearful televised confession where he famously cries, "I have sinned against you, my Lord," he begins his own independent church.

The end cometh: In 1991, Swaggart is arrested by police for soliciting a prostitute, this time in California...while driving his car on the wrong side of the road.

The preacher: Richard Roberts
The bad idea: "Failing an Oral Exam."
Let us pray: A rock singer who dreams of becoming a headliner in Vegas, Richard, son of iconic televangelist Oral Roberts, is awakened one day from a nap by the voice of God telling him to change his ways. He does. Joining his father's ministry, he eventually rises to chairman.

In 2007, Roberts is accused of illegally funneling tax-exempt Oral Roberts University money to a political associate in Tulsa, Oklahoma. He's further accused of using university funds to cover various expenses, including his daughter's private-jet excursion to the Bahamas, a stable of horses held for his children's exclusive use, eleven home-remodeling projects, and various luxury cars. University staffers even claim they've been compelled to do his daughter's homework.

The end cometh: Terming the accusations "extortion," Roberts nonetheless resigns. In 2008, the university names him president emeritus. And by 2009, all legal issues are settled or dismissed.

The preacher: George Alan Rekers
The bad idea: "Rentboy's Long Stroke."
Let us pray: Photographed at Miami International Airport with a young male traveling companion while returning from a ten-day, overseas trip, Christian leader George Alan Rekers denies the youth is anything more than a paid valet.

One important fact missing from that explanation:

The prominent anti-gay activist, scientific advisor to the National Association for Research and Therapy of Homosexuality (NARTH), and cofounder of the conservative Christian Family Research Council, found his "valet" on Rentboy.com, a website known for arranging homosexual hookups. During their jaunt, the escort claims to have provided Rekers with daily nude massages, highlighted by a special technique he dubs "the long stroke."

The end cometh: After protesting, "I deliberately spend time with sinners with the loving goal to try to help them," Rekers nonetheless resigns from NARTH in 2010.

STINKY THINKING from AIR, LAND, & SEA

TEST-DRIVE
the LUXURIOUS NEW FORD LEMON SUCKER

the
BAD IDEA:

The Edsel.

the geniuses
BEHIND IT:

Ford Motor Company
muckety-mucks

the brainstorm
STRUCK:

1957

MICHAEL N. SMITH AND ERIC KASUM

bring on the BLUNDER:

With archrival General Motors taking the pole position in America's big-car sales race, Ford management, despite warnings of an oncoming economic recession, decides to hit the competitive accelerator—investing the then-astonishing sum of $400 million to create "an entirely new kind of car."

Promising revolutionary "You Ideas" (such as a push-button transmission), the Edsel (named after founder Henry Ford's son) is conceived and developed in strict secrecy. It's even shipped to 1,500 new Edsel dealerships under tarps to hide the car's "groundbreaking" design from public view.

from bad TO WORSE:

Then, just as consumer anticipation shifts into high gear, the wheels come off. The eagerly awaited unveiling of the inaugural 1958 Edsel is met with a collective "Ugh!"—as in "ugly." One auto critic sniggers that the car's horse-collar-shaped grill "looks like an Oldsmobile sucking on a lemon." *Consumer Reports* spotlights problems with workmanship. Ford research reveals that recession-wary consumers are resisting the Edsel's high sticker price.

dumb LUCK:

In 1958, Edsel sales drop 30 percent. By 1960, sales plummet 90 percent. After just three model years—and hundreds of million in losses—Ford brings Edsel production to a screeching, merciful, permanent halt.

after THOUGHTS:

One of the greatest commercial missteps of all time, "Edsel" has become synonymous with any bungled new product launch. Ironically, avid collectors today are willing to pay a pretty penny (up to $200,000) for one of these ugly ducklings.

I CAN STOP THIS TRAIN—
& I'M NOT JUST
YANKING YOUR CHAIN

the
BAD
IDEA:

Give passengers
easy access to
a locomotive's
braking system.

the geniuses
BEHIND IT:

The caboose-heads at
the Ministry of Railways,
government of India

the brainstorm
STRUCK:

1853

MICHAEL N. SMITH AND ERIC KASUM

With over 18 million passengers clickety-clacking through nearly 7,000 stations in 28 states, the Indian Railway is one of the busiest rail networks in the world.

Yet despite their practical (not to mention moral) responsibility to deliver passengers safely and efficiently, railway leaders have a head-scratcher of a notion: Give each rider the power to stop the train at will.

**from bad
TO WORSE:**

Simply by pulling a chain situated in the passenger compartment, riders can engage the train's emergency brakes, bringing the speeding locomotive to a screeching stop.

Designed to allow passengers to react to an emergency, chain-pulling soon becomes a national pastime, reported to cause derailments and injuries. What's more, impatient riders are known to pull the chain, halt the train, and disembark before a scheduled station stop—delaying hundreds of fellow passengers forced to sit and wait as a result.

**dumb
LUCK:**

Still rampant on Indian railways, chain-pulling today carries a penalty of 1,000 rupees (about $16) and/or one year's jail time. Responding to the problem, former Indian president A. P. J. Abdul Kalam proposes replacing chain-braking systems with chain alarm systems that alert authorities in case of emergencies—thereby leaving operational control in the hands of the engineer.

**after
THOUGHTS:**

Though never convincingly linked to the Indian Railway problem, "You're yanking my chain" is now a well-known idiom for teasing or kidding.

Oh, THE STUPIDITY!

the BAD IDEA: Cross the ocean beneath a giant tube bursting with highly combustible hydrogen.

the geniuses BEHIND IT:

The Zeppelin Company

the brainstorm STRUCK:

Mid-1930s

bring on the BLUNDER:

In our high-tech era where transatlantic flight is a safe, daily occurrence, it's tough to imagine a time when the most sought-after America-to-Europe airline ticket gave you a seat hung precariously below 7 million cubic feet of volatile, flammable hydrogen.

But in the absence of yet-to-be-created Boeing 747s, gas-filled airships or "dirigibles," such as Germany's *Hindenburg,* are the hip continent-hopper's best alternative to lengthy travel on the high seas—so long as said traveler is comfortable riding a big, bulging fire hazard.

MICHAEL N. SMITH AND ERIC KASUM

from bad TO WORSE:

The year is 1937. Here in its first season of transoceanic flight, the *Hindenburg* completes a Frankfurt-to-Rio round-trip sojourn before lifting off for the United States. Strong headwinds and stormy weather at its Lakehurst, New Jersey, destination push the dirigible and its ninety-seven passengers nearly twelve hours off schedule.

As the airship at last nears its Jersey docking moor, witnesses report that the outer skin above the upper fin begins to flap, as if gas is escaping from inside. At the same time, blue arcs of electricity are seen near the same port fin. Within moments, mushroom-shaped flames engulf the entire zeppelin.

dumb LUCK:

A mere thirty-five seconds later, the *Hindenburg*'s fabric skin is vaporized. As its inner duralumin skeleton crashes feebly to the ground, eyewitness radio reporter Herbert Morrison plaintively cries the now legendary: "Oh, the humanity!" Thirty-five passengers on board—and one person on the ground—perish.

after THOUGHTS:

Was it static electricity? Lightning? A structural failure? Even sabotage? No one knows the true cause of the *Hindenburg* disaster. But one thing is certain: Coupled with the fatal crash of the helium-filled USS *Akron* four years earlier, it spells the end of public confidence in long-range airship travel for good.

Holy Schettino,
HOW DID THAT GUY BECOME A CAPTAIN?

the BAD IDEA:

Steer your cruise ship off course toward a rocky island shore just so that your crew can wave to its homies.

the genius BEHIND IT:

MS *Costa Concordia* Captain Francesco Schettino

the brainstorm STRUCK:

January 13, 2012

bring on the BLUNDER:

The passengers and crew are largely unfazed when their cruise ship, *Costa Concordia*, veers off course and heads for the rocky shoals around Giglio Island, near the coast of Italy.

After all, Captain Francesco Schettino regularly orders "close passes" as a way to show off his huge, glistening, $562 million ship to onshore locales. Plus, it affords Schettino an opportunity to demonstrate his captaining skills to the unauthorized guests he's invited onto the bridge this day.

But among all the frivolity and distractions, the massive ship scrapes into a reef and runs aground. In no time, it takes on water and lists, largely submerged, onto its starboard side. Thirty-two people on board are killed.

In the chaos that follows, Captain Schettino reassures coast guard authorities that his ship has merely temporarily lost power—leaving out the rather important fact that the *Concordia* is currently sinking. Then, consumed with panic, he violates a ship captain's prime maritime directive and abandons his vessel, even as passengers desperately scramble to board lifeboats. He later argues with those same dumbfounded authorities via cell phone when they implore him to return to the ship immediately to coordinate evacuation.

dumb
LUCK:

By the time the saltwater settles, Schettino is charged with manslaughter, among other crimes. Because 2,300 tons of fuel has poured into the Mediterranean from the *Concordia*'s breached hull, he's even charged with destroying a natural habitat: the environmental preserve on Giglio. Megalawsuits, brought by passengers and families of the victims, are also pending against the operators of the ship and its owner, Carnival Corporation of Florida.

after
THOUGHTS:

Despite later telling investigators that he had not been drinking alcohol, the married Schettino is photographed having dinner and a decanter of wine with a young female cruise-ship dancer thirty minutes before the crash. Further compromising his credibility, the captain also claims to have accidentally fallen into a lifeboat when the ship suddenly lurched onto its side prior to sinking. In July 2013, he stands trial on multiple counts of manslaughter.

THEY SING THE BODY ELECTRIC, THEN HUMMER A DIFFERENT TUNE

the BAD IDEA: Pull the plug on a fuel-efficient electric car and instead develop the gas-chugging, pollutant-spewing Hummer.

the geniuses BEHIND IT:

General Motors management

the brainstorm STRUCK:

2003

bring on the BLUNDER:

As Southern California wheezes its way toward the new millennium—with forty-one dangerous stage-one smog alerts in 1995 alone—vehicle-generated air pollution has become nothing to sneeze at.

So the California Air Resources Board adopts a tough law that threatens to block automakers from selling new cars in the state unless they commit to building ZEVs (zero emission vehicles). Viewing this as an SUV-sized assault on the profitable status quo, GM responds by shifting its ZEV project into forward—and also into reverse.

MICHAEL N. SMITH AND ERIC KASUM

**from bad
TO WORSE:**

For starters, GM spends $1 billion developing and marketing the EV1, an electric car that burns no gasoline and emits only water vapor. Meanwhile, the company ponies up millions more to lobby for the ZEV law's repeal. It then punches the accelerator on development of the 6,600-pound, 9.6-miles per gallon (if you're lucky) Hummer.

With GM cash driving the debate, the ZEV law crashes and burns in 2003. In celebration, the automaker recalls—and destroys—all EV1s upon completion of their lease, citing supposed unfixable overheating and fire dangers. It then steers attention to the Hummer sales effort. But the excrement soon hits the radiator fan.

**dumb
LUCK:**

On July 4, 2008, American gasoline prices reach a then-record $4.12 a gallon. Great Recession–strapped Americans turn away from expensive gas-guzzlers, such as the Hummer, and seek out smaller, greener, more fuel-efficient vehicles. Long ago having ceded the small car market to foreign competitors, GM declares bankruptcy less than a year later. Pulling the plug on economical cars like the EV1 has helped short-circuit the world's most powerful automaker.

**after
THOUGHTS:**

Despite GM's efforts, the electric car lives on today. For example, the current-powered Tesla accelerates as fast as a Ferrari (0–60 miles per hour in 3.7 seconds) and can race more than 250 miles on a single battery charge. And Raser H3 has unveiled a newly modified Hummer gas/electric hybrid, which boasts an amazing 100 miles per gallon.

A HORSELESS CARRIAGE *of a* DIFFERENT COLOR?

the BAD IDEA:

The unihue automobile.

the genius BEHIND IT:	Henry Ford

the brainstorm STRUCK:	1908

MICHAEL N. SMITH AND ERIC KASUM

bring on the BLUNDER:

Long before ecru, maize, or topaz, automobiles come in your color choice of black, black, or (if you ask nicely and place your order early) black.

Why the lack of options? Well, according to Ford Motor Company founder Henry Ford, the auto industry's resident übergod, black paint dries more quickly—allowing for the more efficient operation of his revolutionary assembly line.

Most other manufacturers, bowing to Ford's 50 percent market dominance, dutifully follow his lead. And for nearly twenty years, all American-manufactured cars are the same somber color.

from bad TO WORSE:

But over time, by insisting on offering consumers "[a]ny color they like, as long as it's black," Ford inadvertently hands his competition a differentiating edge. Buick, Chevrolet, Oldsmobile, Chrysler, Packard, and others eventually successfully make their autos available in a variety of colors.

dumb LUCK:

As the Great Depression trudges on, Ford's dominant market share begins to drop—never again to approach 50 percent. In 1927, Henry finally relents, allowing his executive team to introduce a new Ford: the Model A. It's available, of course, in a host of colors.

after THOUGHTS:

Henry Ford's obsessive pursuit of efficiency cuts the price of an automobile to just $290, the equivalent of a highly economical $3,258 today. His legendary thrift also leads him to recycle wooden shipping crates from suppliers to make seats for the Model T—and to turn wood scraps from the production of Model Ts into salable charcoal.

UNCOOL *at any* SPEED

the **BAD IDEA:**

The Chevy Corvair.

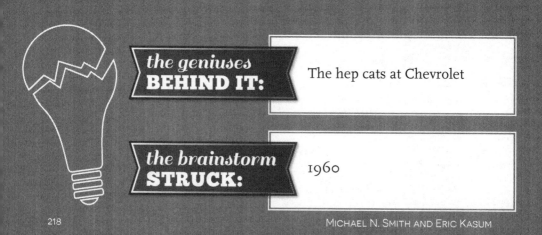

the geniuses **BEHIND IT:**	The hep cats at Chevrolet
the brainstorm **STRUCK:**	1960

MICHAEL N. SMITH AND ERIC KASUM

bring on the BLUNDER:

The marketers at Chevy take one look at the youthful popularity of the Volkswagen Beetle and decide to emulate key features of that novel little auto—its compact size, air-cooled rear engine, and scaled-down transaxle, among others—in designing the company's first "American-sized compact": the Corvair.

With its pioneering unibody construction and optional turbo charger, the Corvair sells more than 250,000 units its first year. Sales continue to accelerate into the mid-1960s—until the power of the pen suddenly causes the car's popularity to hit the skids.

from bad TO WORSE:

In his 1965 book *Unsafe at Any Speed*, consumer activist Ralph Nader zeros in on the car's "swing axle" rear suspension system, exposing how it contributes to loss of driver control, spinouts, and rollovers.

Terming it "the one-car accident," Nader spotlights Chevrolet's cost-cutting measures to the Corvair's suspension, causing it to "tuck under" when strained, often with deadly results.

dumb LUCK:

Facing a front trunk load of negative publicity—not to mention intense competition from the hip, new Ford Mustang—Chevrolet general manager John DeLorean slams on the brakes. He orders production of just 6,000 new Corvairs in what proves to be its final year: 1969.

after THOUGHTS:

Chevrolet's decision to halt the Corvair line comes despite modifications to the suspension system, undertaken in 1964, that all but eliminate tuck-under crashes. Still, it stands as the last rear-engine, air-cooled car made in America.

BLIND AMBITION *meets* HIGHWAY ROBBERY

the BAD IDEA: Trust the Ford Motor Company not to steal your invention.

the genius BEHIND IT:	Inventor Robert Kearns
the brainstorm STRUCK:	December 1, 1964

bring on the BLUNDER:

It's his wedding night. And in a blissful, celebratory moment, Robert Kearns pops a champagne cork—right into his left eye, leaving him partially blind.

Fast-forward ten years. Driving home in a rainstorm, the sight-impaired automotive engineer and part-time inventor squints through his car's rapidly oscillating windshield wipers—and nearly swerves off the road.

Yet even with one bad eye, Kearns sees an opportunity. The result is a visionary invention: the intermittent windshield wiper. And with his newly patented automotive gadget come dreams of fame and riches.

Looking to cash in, Kearns takes his invention to Ford. But while in negotiations, Ford engineers secretly co-opt Kearns's brainchild. Paying him nothing for the rights, they begin to install their own version of his intermittent wipers in Ford models the next year. In the blink of an eye, Chrysler, GM, Mercedes, and Japanese automakers also clone his new invention.

In David-like fashion, Kearns sues the Goliath Ford. Remarkably, he wins, settling for $10.1 million. He then spends all those proceeds (eventually serving as his own lawyer) to sue Chrysler—and is awarded a $30 million judgment.

Sadly, his obsessive, years-long legal battles against Big Auto cost Kearns his career, his marriage, and his health. Long since divorced, blackballed from the auto industry, and living hand to mouth in solitude, he's able to enjoy his legal settlement but a brief time before succumbing to brain cancer in 2005.

If Kearns had been paid just one dollar for each new intermittent wiper system installed from 1970 until the time of his death in 2005, his bright idea would have netted him at least $560 million. A motion picture based on his exploits, *Flash of Genius*, starring Greg Kinnear debuted in 2008.

The Worst of the Worst: Hook, Line, and Sinker

The *Titanic*: One Bad Idea Begets Four Others

On April 14, 1912, the RMS *Titanic*, the fastest and biggest ship on Earth—carrying some of the richest people on Earth—rams an iceberg at full speed and plunges into the icy depths of the North Atlantic. More than 1,700 people die within minutes.

While this disaster has become iconic, its tale is sadly ironic. It's the story of one bad idea leading to another...and another... and another...and, regrettably, another.

👎 Bad Idea 1: Brittle Steel

The steel used in the construction of the *Titanic* is less than optimal, containing high amounts of sulfur. As a result, in the frigid waters of the North Atlantic, the ship's hull becomes increasingly brittle—and all the more vulnerable to perforation by a sharp foreign object—such as an iceberg.

👎 Bad Idea 2: No Roofs

Thomas Andrews, the ship's designer/architect, does not specify that roofs be placed on the "watertight" compartments. As each compartment fills after iceberg impact, water flows over the tops of the walls, flooding the next compartment—

MICHAEL N. SMITH AND ERIC KASUM

and the next and the next—dooming the ship. Roofs could have restrained the flooding water and might have saved the *Titanic*.

👎 Bad Idea 3: Lookouts without Binoculars

On the night of the disaster, lookouts Frederick Fleet and Reginald Lee are high up in the ship's crow's nest, squinting into the darkness in a fruitless effort to spot icebergs. Why? Because someone borrowed their binoculars—and neglected to return them. By the time they spot danger and scream "Iceberg—right ahead!" it's already too late.

👎 Bad Idea 4: Hard-a-Starboard

The moment Fleet and Lee spot the iceberg, First Officer William Murdoch makes a grave mistake: He gives the order to turn the ship "hard-a-starboard" in an effort to avoid the iceberg. This causes the mountain of ice to scrape along the side of the ship's hull, flooding the first five compartments. If Murdoch had simply kept the ship on a straight course, the *Titanic* would have hit the iceberg head-on, crushing only two of its forward compartments. This would have crippled the ship, but experts say the *Titanic* would have survived the impact with virtually no loss of life.

👎 Bad Idea 5: Few Lifeboats

As the vessel dips under the ocean's surface, passengers learn that the *Titanic* carries only enough lifeboats for *half* of all people on board. Result: Over 1,700 people perish, including Captain Edward Smith and ship architect Andrews. Lookout Lee, along with first officer Murdoch, are also lost. But Bruce Ismay, owner of the "unsinkable" *Titanic*, climbs into a lifeboat and saves himself.

MAD
SCIENTISTS
and the
MONSTERS
THEY CREATE

Mr. Cane Toad's
WILD RISE

the BAD IDEA: Import a fat, poisonous, voracious toad to rid your sugar cane crops of pesky beetles.

the geniuses BEHIND IT: Farmers in Cairns, Australia

the brainstorm STRUCK: 1935

bring on the BLUNDER:

A swarm of sweet-toothed beetles is chomping away at Australia's sugar cane crop. So, by cracky, local farmers come up with the perfect solution: Introduce 102 toads from Hawaii to scarf up the bothersome beetle population.

Problem solved, eh, mates? Not quite. Our Outback sugar farmers fail to realize an important rule of amphibious physics: Beetles can scurry safely to the top of a cane plant where the heavy, dinner-plate-sized cane toads can't reach. Thus begins one of the worst ecological calamities in Australian history.

As the cane beetles continue to destroy the sugar crop unchecked, the poisonous toad behemoths eat virtually everything else in sight. Some grow to over two feet in length, tip the scales at more than six pounds, and live up to thirty-five years before croaking.

That's bad, but this is worse: With females producing over 50,000 eggs per year, the cane toads soon displace rabbits as the island nation's biggest pest—found rummaging in home trash cans, bushels of grocery store produce, restaurant pantries, home cupboards, and more. Meanwhile, thanks to their poisonous innards, they cause the death of thousands of birds, snakes, dingoes, and crocs that dine on them.

**dumb
LUCK:**

Today, the Australian cane toad population tops 200 million, with no solution in sight. Recently, a $50 per-toad bounty has been posted. And one of the country's richest men has offered a glass of beer for every bag of dead toads delivered.

**after
THOUGHTS:**

The latest hope for cane toad eradication is a meat-eating ant native to Australia—which can be lured to toad habitats using, of all things, cat food as bait.

THEᴊE DUDES MUᴊT HAVE BEEN HIGH WHEN THEY MADE THIS WEED DEAL

the BAD IDEA:

The genetically modified soybean.

the geniuses BEHIND IT: The weed-whackers at the agricultural biotech giant Monsanto

the brainstorm STRUCK: 1996

bring on the BLUNDER:

Dig this, Mr. Farmer: Monsanto's new genetically altered soy plant is really going to please your bean counters—because it eliminates the enormous costs that go into weeding your fields. As long as you spray your crop with Roundup herbicide (also made by Monsanto), you'll never have to weed again.

So goes Monsanto's pitch to the world's soy farmers, conveniently leaving out one key point: It's all a load of manure.

from bad TO WORSE:

See, once planted, the Monsanto soy requires huge amounts of expensive Roundup to kill nearby weeds. And only Roundup will do. (Cheaper alternative herbicides will poison the crop.) Over time, the cost of Roundup (gee, what a surprise) grows and grows. Also over time, something else begins to grow and grow: new, tougher, Roundup-resistant weeds.

dumb LUCK:

Having been compelled to use Roundup regardless of its rising cost, soy farmers are now forced to spend extra dollars to kill the very weeds the company promised to eradicate.

after THOUGHTS:

Genetically modified organisms are at the center of controversy everywhere today. Advocates claim that they significantly improve crop yields. Detractors claim that GMO foods are untested, unlabeled, and may be unsafe to consume.

By the way, should the wind carry your Monsanto soy pollen to a neighbor's farm, inadvertently cross-pollinating his crop, Monsanto is empowered to demand that your neighbor pitchfork over a per-acre "technology fee."

$\mathcal{O}$ilpocalypse **NOW**

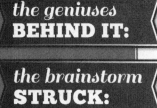

the BAD IDEA: Allow the oil industry to effectively regulate itself.

the geniuses BEHIND IT:

The U.S. Minerals Management Service

the brainstorm STRUCK:

1982 to present

bring on the BLUNDER:

Let's say you're a border patrol agent, duty-bound to stop and inspect vehicles for illegal contraband. Now let's say you also collect a fee from each automobile you allow to pass over the border.

That would be a rather absurd conflict of interest—one that couldn't happen in the real world, right? Wrong, slick. You've just entered the greasy world of the U.S. Minerals Management Service, where the cop in charge of shutting down unsafe oil wells is the same guy who makes gushers of money when the wells keep flowing strong.

MICHAEL N. SMITH AND ERIC KASUM

How's it work? The MMS outlines broad safety goals for the dangerous business of drilling for oil. It then permits the industry to come up with its own strategies for achieving those goals—with minimal oversight. At the same time, MMS collects revenue from oil companies who drill on government property.

dumb
LUCK:

Result A: Safety features, such as "blowout preventers," are meekly suggested by regulators, then summarily ignored by oil drillers.

Result B: An offshore oil worker in the United States today is four times more likely to be killed on the job than one in Europe, where safety enforcement and royalty collections are supervised by separate entities.

Result C: The Deepwater Horizon blast that kills eleven workers while spewing an estimated 4.9 million barrels of crude into the Gulf of Mexico over a three-month period in 2009. It's the largest offshore oil disaster in U.S. history.

after
THOUGHTS:

In 2008, MMS employees are found to have created a "culture of ethical failure" by accepting gifts from— and having sex with—oil and mineral industry representatives. In 2009, Donald C. Howard, the former MMS Gulf of Mexico regional supervisor, pleads guilty to lying about gifts he received.

Then, in 2012, oil giant BP is hit with the largest criminal fine in U.S. history as part of a $4.5 billion settlement in the fatal Deepwater Horizon disaster. The Obama administration implements environmental reviews for all new deep-water oil drilling, ending the kind of exemptions that had allowed BP to drill in the Gulf of Mexico with little scrutiny.

ATTACK *of* the FRANKENFISH

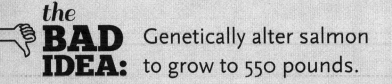

the BAD IDEA: Genetically alter salmon to grow to 550 pounds.

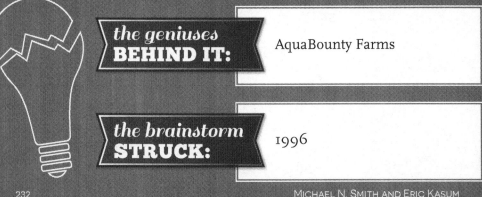

the geniuses BEHIND IT: AquaBounty Farms

the brainstorm STRUCK: 1996

MICHAEL N. SMITH AND ERIC KASUM

bring on the BLUNDER:

The typical salmon: He's about twenty pounds, loves to swim upstream, and tastes pinky good when broiled or poached.

But same-old Sal just isn't good enough for Canadian-based AquaBounty Farms. It applies to the U.S. Food and Drug Administration for permission to create a genetically modified super salmon: one that grows seven times faster, resists most diseases, and attracts more mates than Paris Hilton.

But before the company's finned version of Fat Bastard ever hits the water, reality casts its net.

from bad TO WORSE:

Terming the new farm-raised salmon "Frankenfish," biologists and fishermen's groups raise concerns that the super salmon might escape and carry "Trojan horse genes" into wild salmon populations, causing mutations, disease, even death.

The bigger, faster, sexier, new fish might wipe out the nation's already extinction-threatened salmon stocks, they fear. Or become a supersized disease carrier.

dumb LUCK:

In the face of this outcry, the FDA denies AquaBounty's request. But like Jason, Frankenfish are hard to kill. Worry persists that other interested countries—most notably China and Russia—will approve the transgenic salmon in the years ahead.

after THOUGHTS:

Research on some thirty-five species of transgenic fish is under way worldwide, including striped bass, rainbow trout, catfish, and tilapia, as well as abalone and oysters.

The PESTICIDE THAT COMMITS HOMICIDE

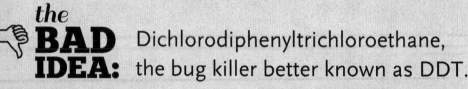

the BAD IDEA: Dichlorodiphenyltrichloroethane, the bug killer better known as DDT.

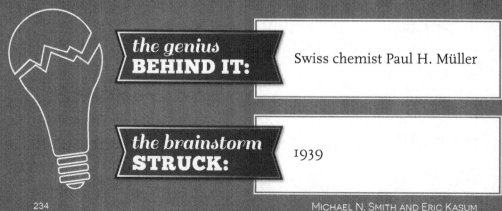

the genius BEHIND IT: Swiss chemist Paul H. Müller

the brainstorm STRUCK: 1939

MICHAEL N. SMITH AND ERIC KASUM

**bring on the
BLUNDER:**

They're the ultimate buzzkill. Malaria-carrying mosquitoes murder millions of people each year.

Swiss chemist Paul Müller and his pesticide DDT to the rescue. Immediately hailed as the antidote to the scourge of bug-borne diseases, 3.6 billion pounds of DDT are sprayed across the globe during the 1940s and 1950s—all without regard for the deadly, long-lasting chemical's potential side effects on plant, animal, and human life.

**from bad
TO WORSE:**

Over the years, those troublesome problems create a buzz of their own. DDT is blamed for sizable declines in global bird populations, including the iconic bald eagle. Rachel Carson's 1962 book *Silent Spring* posits a time when DDT has forever quieted the sound of birds and insects—turning forests and beaches into still, barren wastelands.

**dumb
LUCK:**

Worse yet, scientists find that the latest generation of mosquitoes has grown resistant to DDT exposure—even as fish and animals continue to die from its onerous effects.

By 1972, with evidence mounting of DDT's role in causing deadly cancers, diabetes, asthma, and various neurological disorders in humans, the same chemical that won Müller the 1948 Nobel Prize for Medicine (yes, *medicine*) is forever banned in the United States.

**after
THOUGHTS:**

A testament to its extraordinary staying power, virtually every American today is thought to have poisonous DDT in his or her bloodstream—over four decades after its prohibition.

More of the Best of the Worst: Bad Ideas Gone Good

👍 Blind Teen Creates an Awl-Some Invention

Louis, a three-year-old French boy, plays with a sharp, pointed awl. Bad idea. He accidentally lances his eye, causing an infection that leaves him totally blind.

But that unfortunate childhood accident inspires Louis, now thirteen, to use the same type of awl that caused his blindness to create a raised-dot, touch-based reading system that gains worldwide acceptance and today carries his now-famous surname: Braille.

👍 A Forgettable Film Leads to an Unforgettable Rescue

Movie actor Ronald Reagan calls his 1939 movie *The Code of the Secret Service* one of his most forgettable films. With a loopy plot about strange Mexican counterfeiters, it's a bad cinematic idea.

But this subpar movie motivates a young Miami boy named Jerry Parr to become a Secret Service agent himself. Years later, Agent Parr braves a hail of assassin's bullets to sweep a wounded U.S. president into the safety of his waiting limo and off to a nearby hospital. The president whose life Parr helped save? Former *Code* star Ronald Reagan.

MICHAEL N. SMITH AND ERIC KASUM

👍 An Upchuck of Historic Proportions

On board a small ship in one of the biggest storms of 1620, a young man named John Howland has a not-so-bright idea: Seasick, he decides to lean far over the ship's railing to vomit—and is immediately swept overboard. Surfacing momentarily in the roiling ocean, he gasps for breath, spots a halyard rope bobbing nearby, grabs it, and is ultimately pulled safely back on deck by fellow passengers.

Howland, you'll note, is a pilgrim. The ship is the *Mayflower*. And his heart-stopping rescue at sea has caught the eye of a beautiful young shipmate named Elizabeth Tilley. The two eventually marry. Together, they make lots of babies—ten in all. And those kiddies make history. Howland's descendants include presidents Franklin D. Roosevelt, George H. W. Bush, and George W. Bush; actors Humphrey Bogart and Alec Baldwin; and Joseph Smith, founder of the Mormon Church.

👍 A Not-So-Sticky Situation

Spencer Silver, a scientist for the 3M Company, in 1970 sets out to create a better adhesive. Instead, he inadvertently formulates a weak adhesive that doesn't stick very well. On paper, it's a bad idea.

But this poor adhesive sticks in the mind of another 3M scientist, Arthur Fry. One Sunday, while opening his church hymnbook, the torn pieces of paper he uses as bookmarks fall to the floor.

Like a bolt from above, he remembers the not-so-sticky glue and comes up with the concept for notepaper that can be stuck, removed, and restuck as needed. Nine years later, the now-hugely popular Post-it Notes are born.

👍 He Forgets His Underwear and Turns Blue

A young man named Strauss hits San Francisco in 1853 with dreams of opening his own dry goods business—selling such things as umbrellas, handkerchiefs, and underwear. In brief (or should we say "briefs"?), not a great idea. Competition in Gold Rush Northern California is brisk. And many a boom-town business fails.

Yet Strauss recognizes an opportunity. Given the rigors of panning for gold, prospectors quickly wear through the thin fabric of their trousers. Tailoring tent canvas, Strauss and partner Jacob Davis respond by inventing the strong, durable outerwear that comes to be known as blue jeans. Today, more than 150 years later, those same tough, stylish pants bear Strauss's first name: Levi.

👍 A Golden Moldy

Bacteriologist Alexander Fleming, experimenting in 1928 with staphylococci, inadvertently leaves a set of laboratory dishes brimming with staph bacteria by an open window. Dumb idea. Not surprisingly, mold blows in from an outside garden and contaminates the dishes.

But Fleming has a healthy curiosity. He decides to examine the contaminated dishes, quickly noting that the mold is eating the bacteria. Fleming's open window has opened the door to the discovery of penicillin. And thanks to this "happy accident," millions of lives are saved over the next eight decades.

MICHAEL N. SMITH AND ERIC KASUM

ACKNOWLEDGMENTS

The authors would like to thank Gutenberg for inventing the printing press, Berners-Lee for helping invent the worldwide web, Debora Smith for her editing and proofreading prowess, Scott Marsh for his artistic eye, Marah Cannon for her dogged insistence that we get the book finished, Jill Marsal for her steadfast belief in us, and our new friends at Sourcebooks for their tireless enthusiasm and support. Oh, and let's not forget all the well-intended but ultimately ill-fated historical screwups who made all this silly fun possible.

A OUT THE AUT ORS

SIMON NASH STUDIOS

Michael N. Smith, as owner of his own advertising production company, has written and produced hundreds of humorous (and not-so-humorous) TV commercials, radio spots, and corporate videos over the past twenty-five years for a gaggle of clients across our great land. His work has garnered numerous honors, including CLIO, ADDY, EFFIE, New York Art Directors, and TELLY awards. He also created the popular cult comic book character Pete the P.O.'d Postal Worker as well as a children's book parody by the same name. He's penned features for *National Lampoon, National Geographic Kids, Men's Exercise*, the *Orange County Register*, the *Los Angeles Times*, the *Buffalo News*, the *St. Petersburg Times*, and the *San Antonio Express News*. Mike kids history, but always with love. He lives with his wife, Debora, and son, Andrew, in California.

Eric Kasum wrote speeches for former president George H. W. Bush as well as President Ronald Reagan's White House Chief of Staff and former attorney general Edwin Meese. As a journalist, he wrote for the *Los Angeles Times*, the *New York Times Magazine* group, and CBS News. Eric also wrote for a respected think tank in Washington, DC. He is founder and CEO of the Imagine Institute, a think tank for peace, and host of the Imagine Peace Conference at UC Berkeley. His work has appeared in the *Huffington Post* as well as more than one hundred newspapers and magazines around the world. He lives in California.

BIBLIOGRAPHY

The President's Scandalous Em-Bare-Ass-Ment

"John Quincy Adams: Skinny Dipping & Other Firsts." HistoryofOld.com, August 21, 2011. www.historyofold.com/2011/08/john-quincy-adams-skinny-dipping-other.html (accessed August 25, 2013).

"President's Korner: The John Quincy Adams Nude Bathing Story." *Huffington Post*, October 24, 2012. www.huffingtonpost.com/2012/10/24/john-quincy-adams-nude-bathing_n_2010866.html (accessed August 25, 2013).

Beyer, Rick. *The Greatest Presidential Stories Never Told: 100 Tales from History to Astonish, Bewilder, and Stupefy.* New York: Collins, 2007.

Wiseman, Rachel. "The Unabridged (But Sadly Unillustrated) History of Political Skinny-Dipping." *New Republic*, August 20, 2012. www.newrepublic.com/blog/plank/106331/brief-unillustrated-history-skinny-dipping-politicians (accessed August 25, 2013).

Why Is Dumbo Wearing Hiking Boots?

Hoyte, John. *Trunk Road for Hannibal: With an Elephant Over the Alps.* London: G. Bles, 1960.

Lendering, Jona. "Hannibal." Livius: Articles on Ancient History. www.livius.org/ha-hd/hannibal/hannibal.html (accessed August 6, 2013).

Thiess, Anne, and Walter Thiess. *Hannibal.* New York: Funk & Wagnalls, 1968.

A Confused Chauffeur Starts a World War

Dash, Mike. "Gavrilo Princip's Sandwich." *Smithsonian.com*, September 15, 2011. blogs.smithsonianmag.com/history/2011/09/gavrilo-princips-sandwich/ (accessed August 6, 2013).

Duffy, Michael. "Archduke Franz Ferdinand." Firstworldwar.com, August 22, 2009. www.firstworldwar.com/bio/ferdinand.htm (accessed August 6, 2013).

Remak, Joachim. *Sarajevo: The Story of a Political Murder.* New York: Criterion Books, 1959.

The Great Leap Forward Falls on Its Face

Dikötter, Frank. *Mao's Great Famine: The History of China's Most Devastating Catastrophe, 1958–1962.* New York: Walker & Co., 2010.

Southerland, Daniel. "Repression's Higher Toll: New Evidence Shows Famine, Violence Spared Few." *Washington Post*, July 17, 1994.

Várdy, Steven Béla, and Agnes Huszár Várdy. "Cannibalism in Stalin's Russia and Mao's China." *East European Quarterly* 41, no. 2 (Summer 2007): 223-238.

Yang, Jisheng. *Tombstone: The Untold Story of Mao's Great Famine.* Trans. Stacy Mosher and Guo Jian. London: Allen Lane, 2012.

Pay Me Now or I'll Splay You Later

"Vortigern." Wikipedia. en.wikipedia.org/wiki/Vortigern (accessed August 18, 2013).

Castleden, Rodney. *King Arthur: The Truth Behind the Legend*. London: Routledge, 2000.

Henshall, Kenneth G. *Folly and Fortune in Early British History: From Caesar to the Normans*. Basingstoke, UK: Palgrave Macmillan, 2008.

Laycock, Stuart. *Warlords: The Struggle for Power in Post-Roman Britain*. Stroud, UK: The History Press, 2009.

Shore, Thomas William. *Origin of the Anglo-Saxon Race: A Study of the Settlement of England and the Tribal Origin of the Old English People*. 1906. Reprint Port Washington, NY: Kennikat Press, 1971.

Tippecanoe and Prez for a Month Too

"More Tales from the Crypt." *The Economist* 319 (June 22, 1991): 35.

Beyer, Rick. *The Greatest Presidential Stories Never Told: 100 Tales from History to Astonish, Bewilder, and Stupefy*. New York: Collins, 2007.

Collins, Gail. "William Henry Harrison." *Washington Post*, March 19, 2012.

Kauffman, Bill. "He Died of the Presidency." *American Enterprise*, April 1, 2006.

Spitzer, Robert J. "Accidental Presidents: Death, Assassination, Resignation, and Democratic Succession." *Presidential Studies Quarterly*, June 1, 2010.

Friday the 13th: The Original Horror Story

"Friday the 13th—Curse or Myth?" *Pueblo Chieftain*, July 14, 2007.

"The Knights Templar." New Advent Catholic Encyclopedia. www.newadvent.org/cathen/14493a.htm (accessed August 20, 2013).

Dafoe, Stephen. "History of the Knights Templar." Templarhistory.com. templarhistory.com/ (accessed August 20, 2013).

Lachenmeyer, Nathaniel. *13: The Story of the World's Most Notorious Superstition*. New York: Plume, 2005.

Preventing 9/11 Could Have Been an Open-and-Shut Case

"Indictment of Zacarias Moussaoui." U.S. Department of Justice. www.justice.gov/ag/ That moussaouiindictment.htm (accessed August 20, 2013).

"Testimony of F.B.I. Agent Harry Samit in the Zacarias Moussaoui Trial." University of Missouri-Kansas City School of Law. law2.umkc.edu/faculty/projects/ftrials/moussaoui/zmsamit.html (accessed August 20, 2013).

"United States of America vs. Zacarias Moussaoui." *CNN.com*. i.a.cnn.net/cnn/2005/images/04/22/moussaoui.statement.pdf (accessed August 17, 2013).

Serrano, Richard A. "9/11 Trial Reveals Troubles Then, and Ahead." *Los Angeles Times*, March 26, 2006. articles.latimes.com/2006/mar/26/nation/na-samit26 (accessed August 20, 2013).

The Assassin's Gunshot That Backfires Big Time

"John Wilkes Booth." Answers.com. www.answers.com/topic/john-wilkes-booth (accessed August 25, 2013).

Kauffman, Michael W. *American Brutus: John Wilkes Booth and the Lincoln Conspiracies*. New York: Random House, 2004.

Sure, He Was a Murdering Marauder, but At Least We Get a Day Off

Columbus, Christopher. "Letter to Luis de Santangel Regarding the First Voyage." In *The Norton Anthology of American Literature*, edited by Nina Baym, 5th ed. New York: W. W. Norton, 1998.

de Las Casas, Bartoleme. "Brief Account of the Devastation of the Indies." Swarthmore College. www.swarthmore.edu/SocSci/bdorsey1/41docs/02-las.html (accessed August 25, 2013).

Frazier, Wade. "Columbus, The Original American Hero." The Home Page of Wade Frazier. www.ahealedplanet.net/columbus.htm (accessed August 26, 2013).

Kasum, Eric. "Columbus Day? True Legacy: Cruelty and Slavery." *Huffington Post*, October 11, 2010. www.huffingtonpost.com/eric-kasum/columbus-day-a-bad-idea_b_742708.html (accessed August 26, 2013).

Sale, Kirkpatrick. *The Conquest of Paradise: Christopher Columbus and the Columbian Legacy*. New York: Knopf, 1990.

Vaughn, Leroy. *Black People & Their Place In World History*. Vol. III, *After 1492 (Columbus)*. www.computerhealth.org/ebook/1492post.htm (accessed August 26, 2013).

By George, That Library Book Is 80,665 Days Late

"George Washington's 221-Year Overdue Library Book: A Timeline." *The Week*, May 21, 2010. theweek.com/article/index/203282/george-washingtons-221-year-overdue-library-book-a-timeline (accessed August 29, 2013).

Boyle, Christina. "Book That George Washington Borrowed from New York Library Is Returned—221 Years Later." *NY Daily News*, May 19, 2010. www.nydailynews.com/new-york/book-george-washington-borrowed-new-york-library-returned-221-years-article-1.448238 (accessed August 29, 2013).

Shapiro, Rich. "President George Washington Racks Up $300,000 Late Fee for Two Manhattan Library Books." *NY Daily News*, April 16, 2010. www.nydailynews.com/new-york/president-george-washington-racks-300-000-late-fee-manhattan-library-books-article-1.170174 (accessed August 29, 2013).

Bones of Contention Pilt on a Lie

"Piltdown Man Is Revealed As Fake." *PBS.org*. www.pbs.org/wgbh/aso/databank/entries/do53pi.html (accessed September 1, 2013).

Blinderman, Charles. *The Piltdown Inquest*. Buffalo, NY: Prometheus Books, 1986.

Harter, Richard. "Piltdown Man." *Real News 24/7*. www.realnews247.com/piltdown_man.htm (accessed September 1, 2013).

Russell, Miles. *Piltdown Man: The Secret Life of Charles Dawson*. Stroud, UK: Tempus, 2003.

If You're Anti-Nuke, This Will Really Hit Your Hot Button

"We Begin Bombing in Five Minutes." Wikipedia. www.en.wikipedia.org/wiki/We_begin_bombing_in_five_minutes (accessed September 1, 2013).

Burr, William. "The 3 A.M. Phone Call." The National Security Archive, March 1, 2012. www2.gwu.edu/~nsarchiv/nukevault/ebb371/ (accessed September 1, 2013).

Fischer, Benjamin B. "A Cold War Conundrum: The 1983 Soviet War Scare." U.S. Central Intelligence Agency. https://www.cia.gov/library/center-for-the-study-of-intelligence/csi-publications/books-and-monographs/a-cold-war-conundrum/source.htm (accessed August 31, 2013).

Forden, Geoffrey. "Reducing a Common Danger: Improving Russia's Early-Warning System." *Policy Analysis* 399 (May 3, 2001). www.cato.org/sites/cato.org/files/pubs/pdf/pa399.pdf (accessed August 31, 2013).

Lewis, Jeffrey. "Nightmare on Nuke Street." *Foreign Policy*, October 30, 2012. www.foreignpolicy.com/articles/2012/10/30/nightmare_on_nuke_street (accessed September 1, 2013).

The Midnight Walk of Paul Revere

"Israel Bissell Outrode Paul Revere, Yet Didn't Get a Poem." *WHDH.com*, April 14, 2007. www4.whdh.com/news/articles/local/BO49091/ (accessed September 1, 2013).

"The Midnight Ride of Israel Bissell." The Red Pill Blog, March 5, 2010. www.multimediaredpill.blogspot.com/2010/03/midnight-ride-of-israel-bissell.html (accessed September 1, 2013).

Bell, J. L. "'Israel Bissell's Ride' and 'I. Bissell's Ride.'" 150 Years of "Paul Revere's Ride." www.paulreveresride.org/2010/03/israel-bissells-ride-and-i-bissells.html (accessed September 1, 2013).

Captured Slave Ship Sets the Abolitionist Movement Free

Amistad. Film. Directed by Steven Spielberg. United States: DreamWorks, 1997.

"Amistad Case." Answers.com. www.answers.com/topic/amistad-1841 (accessed August 31, 2013).

Cable, Mary. *Black Odyssey: The Case of the Slave Ship Amistad*. New York: Viking Press, 1971.

How to Lip-Sink a Music Career

"Milli Vanilli." MTV.com. www.mtv.com/music/artist/milli_vanilli/artist.jhtml (accessed August 6, 2013).

"Milli Vanilli Pair Loses Grammy." *Chicago Sun-Times*, November 20, 1990.

Philips, Chuck. "Milli Vanilli's Grammy Rescinded by Academy: Music: Organization Revokes an Award for the First Time after Revelation That the Duo Never Sang on Album." *Los Angeles Times*, November 20, 1990. www.articles.latimes.com/1990-11-20/news/mn-4948_1_milli-vanilli (accessed August 5, 2013).

E.T.'s Mission to Mars Aborted

Bailey, Jee. "So You Wanna Be In Pictures; Marketing Gurus Share Their Hollywood Strategies for Product Placement." *Daily News Record*, August 25, 2003.

Lovell, Glenn. "Reese's Pieces to Ray-Ban: Memorable Placements." *Knight Ridder/Tribune News Service*, December 26, 1997.

Mikkelson, Barbara. "Taking it E.T." Snopes.com. www.snopes.com/business/market/mandms.asp (accessed August 18, 2013).

Paul, Noel C. "What You See Is What They Want You to Get: Ever since 'E.T.' Landed, Advertisers Have Been Hungry to Have Their Products 'Placed' in Films." *Christian Science Monitor*, April 16, 2002.

Surowiecki, James. "Chocolate Wars." Review of *The Emperors of Chocolate: Inside the Secret World of Hershey and Mars*, by Joel Glenn Brenner. *The Washington Monthly* 31, no. 4 (April 1999).

G-Men Go Screwy Screwy over "Louie Louie"

"High School Band Barred From Playing 'Louie Louie.'" *Music Trades*, July 1, 2005.

"Louie Louie." Snopes.com. www.snopes.com/music/songs/louie.asp (accessed August 18, 2013).

"The Dope on the Unintelligible Classic 'Louie Louie.'" *Seattle Post-Intelligencer*, June 22, 2000.

Harrington, Richard. "Famous Lost Words; How 'Louie Louie's' Unintelligible Lyrics Won Millions of Hearts." *Washington Post*, February 2, 1997.

Hyatt, Josh. "'Louie Louie' the Book—It's Gotta Go." *Boston Globe*, August 9, 1993.

Marsh, Dave. *Louie Louie: The History and Mythology of the World's Most Famous Rock 'n Roll Song*. Ann Arbor: University of Michigan Press, 2010.

Remember the Dorks, Luke

"All Time Box Office Worldwide Grosses." Box Office Mojo. www.boxofficemojo.com/alltime/world/ (accessed August 19, 2013).

"Biography for George Lucas." IMDb. www.imdb.com/name/nm0000184/bio (accessed August 19, 2013).

"Franchises: Star Wars." Box Office Mojo. www.boxofficemojo.com/franchises/chart/?id=starwars.htm (accessed August 19, 2013).

"List of Highest-Grossing Films." Wikipedia. www.en.wikipedia.org/wiki/List_of_highest-grossing_films (accessed August 19, 2013).

"Movie Budget Records." The Numbers. www.the-numbers.com/movies/records/budgets.php (accessed August 19, 2013).

"Star Wars." Box Office Mojo. www.boxofficemojo.com/movies/?id=starwars4.htm (accessed August 19, 2013).

"Star Wars: Episode IV—A New Hope: Trivia." IMDb. www.imdb.com/title/tt0076759/trivia (accessed August 19, 2013).

"The 50th Academy Awards (1978) Nominees and Winners." Academy of Motion Picture Arts and Sciences. www.oscars.org/awards/academyawards/legacy/ceremony/50th-winners.html (accessed August 17, 2013).

Jackson, Matthew. "Studio Execs Didn't Like E.T. + 12 More Sci-Fi Classics." Blastr.com. www.blastr.com/2013-4-26/why-studio-execs-didnt-et-12-more-sci-fi-classics (accessed August 19, 2013).

Don't Tase Me, Bro—(and Don't Sing to Me Either)

"ABC Cancels 'Cop Rock.'" *New York Times*, November 13, 1990. www.nytimes.com/1990/11/13/arts/abc-cancels-cop-rock.html (accessed August 19, 2013).

"Cop Rock." IMDb. www.imdb.com/title/tt0098772/ (accessed August 19, 2013).

"Cop Rock." Television Heaven. www.televisionheaven.co.uk/coprock.htm (accessed August 19, 2013).

"Cop Rock." TV.com. www.tv.com/shows/cop-rock/ (accessed August 19, 2013).

"The Worst TV Shows Ever." *CBSNews.com*, February 11, 2009. www.cbsnews.com/stories/2002/07/12/ entertainment/main515057.shtml (accessed August 19, 2013).

Tucker, Ken. "Review—Flops 101: Lessons from the Biz." *Entertainment Weekly*, June 4, 2004. www .ew.com/ew/article/0,,643229,00.html (accessed August 19, 2013).

Britney Bares All

Knudsen, Michael. "Britney Spears' Crotch Picture Wrap-Up." PopBytes, December 3, 2006. www.popbytes. com/britney_spears_crotch_pussy_no_panties_shot_picture_wrap_up/ (accessed September 19, 2013).

Marikar, Sheila. "Bald and Broken: Inside Britney's Shaved Head." *ABCNews.com*, February 19, 2007. www.abcnews.go.com/Entertainment/Health/story?id=2885048&page=1%20-%20 .TriuOEa0kUU (accessed September 19, 2013).

Nudd, Tim. "Britney's Album Expected to Hit No. 1." *People.com*, November 1, 2007. www.people .com/people/article/0,,20156140,00.html (accessed September 19, 2013).

Springer, John. "Britney's Bald Head: Cry for Help?" *TODAY.com*, February 20, 2007. www.today.com/ id/17226738/%20-%20.TriulEa0kUU#.Ujqex9JzGSo (accessed September 19, 2013).

Look, Dear, Charlie Chaplin Dropped By for a Sleepover

Griffith, Carson. "'Iron Man' Actor Robert Downey Jr. Tells Rolling Stone About Prison, Heroin, Cocaine and the Future." *NY Daily News*, April 28, 2010. www.articles.nydailynews.com/2010-04-29/ gossip/27062936_1_downey-plans-iron-man-coke (accessed August 26, 2013).

Kirn, Walter. "The Tao of Robert Downey Jr." *Rolling Stone*, April 29, 2010. www.rollingstone .com/movies/news/the-tao-of-robert-downey-jr-the-new-issue-of-rolling-stone-20100429 (accessed August 26, 2013).

Pomerantz, Dorothy. "Robert Downey Jr. Tops Forbes' List of Hollywood's Highest-Paid Actors." *Forbes.com*, July 16, 2013. www.forbes.com/sites/dorothypomerantz/2013/07/16/robert-downey-jr-tops-forbes-list-of-hollywoods-highest-paid-actors/ (accessed August 26, 2013).

Reaves, Jessica. "Will Robert Downey Jr.'s Case Spark a Change in Drug Sentencing?" *TIME.com*, February 7, 2001. www.time.com/time/nation/article/0,8599,98373,00.html (accessed August 26, 2013).

Smokey, Not Stirred

"Burt Reynolds." IMDb. www.imdb.com/name/nm0000608/?ref_=fn_al_nm_1 (accessed August 29, 2013).

"Reynolds Still Regrets James Bond Snub." Contactmusic.com, August 1, 2005. www.contactmusic .com/news-article/reynolds-still-regrets-james-bond-snub (accessed August 29, 2013).

Reynolds, Burt. *My Life*. New York: Hyperion, 1994.

Capone's Treasure Turns into Trash TV

"Geraldo Rivera Opens Up Al Capone's Safe On Live TV." WorldHistoryProject.org. www. worldhistoryproject.org/1986/4/21/geraldo-rivera-opens-up-al-capones-safe-on-live-tv (accessed August 29, 2013).

"The Mystery of Al Capone's Vaults." IMDb. www.imdb.com/title/tt0435702/ (accessed August 29, 2013).

"The Mystery of Al Capone's Vaults." Wikipedia. www.en.wikipedia.org/wiki/The_Mystery_of_Al_ Capone%27s_Vault (accessed August 29, 2013).

Dinosaur Helps Bring Actor's Finances to the Brink of Extinction

"Nicolas Cage." AskMen.com. www.askmen.com/celebs/men/entertainment/27_nicolas_cage.html (accessed August 29, 2013).

"Nicolas Cage Outbid Leonardo DiCaprio for a $276,000 Dinosaur Skull." *Us Weekly*, November 9, 2009. www.usmagazine.com/celebrity-news/news/nic-cage-2009911 (accessed August 29, 2013).

Duke, Alan. "Nicolas Cage Caused His Own Financial Ills, Ex-Business Manager Says." *CNN.com*, November 18, 2009. www.cnn.com/2009/SHOWBIZ/11/17/nicolas.cage.lawsuit/index. html?_s=PM:SHOWBIZ (accessed August 29, 2013).

Pete Does His Best to Avoid the Long and Winding Road to Superstardom

"Pete Best Portfolio." The Internet Beatles Album. www.beatlesagain.com/bpete.html (accessed August 30, 2013).

Norman, Philip. *Shout! The True Story of the Beatles*. New York: Simon & Schuster, 1981.

Raiders of the Lost Part

"Heart Beat." IMDb. www.imdb.com/title/tt0080854/ (accessed August 30, 2013).

"Nick Nolte Passed on 'Indiana Jones' and 'Star Wars.'" XFINITY. www.xfinity.comcast.net/slideshow/ entertainment-passedfailed/14/ (accessed August 30, 2013).

Ted Danson's Minstrel Cramp

Staples, Brent. "Manhattan Minstrel Show." *New York Times*, October 13, 1993. www.nytimes. com/1993/10/13/opinion/manhattan-minstrel-show.html (accessed September 1, 2013).

Tucker, Neely. "Hollywood's About-Face on Blackface." *Washington Post*, March 16, 2008. www. washingtonpost.com/wp-dyn/content/article/2008/03/14/AR2008031401124.html (accessed September 1, 2013).

Snuff Daddy's Greatest Hit

"Keith Richards Says He Snorted Father's Ashes." *TODAY.com*, April 4, 2007. www.today.com/ id/17933669/ns/today-entertainment/t/keith-richards-says-hesnorted-fathers-ashes/ (accessed September 1, 2013).

Smith, Graham. "High Life as a Rolling Stone: Keith Richards Reveals All About Drugs, Sex...and Legendary Lover Mick Jagger's 'Tiny' Manhood." *Daily Mail Online*, October 15, 2010. www.dailymail.co.uk/tvshowbiz/article-1320761/Rolling-Stone-Keith-Richards-reveals-drugs-sex-Mick-Jaggers-tiny-manhood.html (accessed September 1, 2013).

Cousin Eddie Checks In, but He Doesn't Check Out

"Randy Quaid News." *TMZ.com*. www.tmz.com/person/randy-quaid/2/ (accessed August 30, 2013).

Hammel, Sara. "Inside Story: Randy Quaid's Journey from Actor to Alleged Felon." *People.com*, November 8, 2009. www.people.com/people/article/0,,20316329,00.html (accessed August 30, 2013).

Dr. Dude Little

"Ken Atison Seiuli." Findadeath.com. www.findadeath.com/Deceased/s/atisonseiuli/seiuli.htm (accessed September 1, 2013).

Ebner, Mark, and Jack Cheevers. "The Bagman." *New Times LA*, April 26, 2001. www .hollywoodinterrupted.com/archives/the_bagman.phtml (accessed September 1, 2013).

Smith, Kyle. "Double Trouble: A Pickup Turns into a Drag for Eddie Murphy." *People.com*, May 19, 1997. www.people.com/people/archive/article/0,,20122170,00.html (accessed September 1, 2013).

Fail to the Chief: Five of the Worst Ideas in Presidential History

"The Iran-Contra Affair." *PBS.org*. www.pbs.org/wgbh/americanexperience/features/general-article/ reagan-iran/ (accessed August 30, 2013).

Chait, Jonathan. "Yes, Bush v. Gore Did Steal the Election." *New York Magazine*, June 25, 2012. nymag .com/daily/intelligencer/2012/06/yes-bush-v-gore-did-steal-the-election.html (accessed August 30, 2013).

Dallek, Robert. "How Not to End Another President's War (L.B.J. Edition)." *New York Times*, March 12, 2009. www.100days.blogs.nytimes.com/2009/03/12/how-not-to-end-another-presidents- war-lbj-edition/?_r=0 (accessed August 29, 2013).

Keating, Robert C. "Most Corrupt Administrations in U.S. History." MostCorrupt.com. mostcorrupt .com/Most-Corrupt-Administrations.html (accessed August 30, 2013).

Kornbluh, Peter, and Malcolm Byrne. "Iran-Contra at 25: Reagan and Bush 'Criminal Liability' Evaluation." The National Security Archive, November 25, 2011. www2.gwu.edu/~nsarchiv/ NSAEBB/NSAEBB365/ (accessed August 30, 2013).

McElvaine, Robert S. *The Great Depression: America, 1929-1941*. New York: Time Books, 1984.

Palast, Greg. "Ex-Con Game: How Florida's 'Felon' Voter-Purge Was Itself Felonious." *Harper's Magazine*, March 1, 2002. www.diggers.org/freecitynews/_disc1/0000001e.htm (accessed August 30, 2013).

Smith, Gene. *The Shattered Dream: Herbert Hoover and the Great Depression*. New York: Morrow, 1970.

Weiner, Rachel. "O'Connor: Maybe Supreme Court Shouldn't Have Taken Bush v. Gore." *Washington Post*, April 29, 2013. www.washingtonpost.com/blogs/post-politics/wp/2013/04/29/oconnor- maybe-supreme-court-shouldnt-have-taken-bush-v-gore/ (accessed August 30, 2013).

The Butt of a Fat Joke

"How Does Olestra Work?" How Stuff Works. www.howstuffworks.com/question526.htm (accessed September 3, 2013).

"Olestra." Wikipedia. www.en.wikipedia.org/wiki/Olestra (accessed September 5, 2013).

"The Facts about Olestra." Center for Science in the Public Interest. www.cspinet.org/olestra/ (accessed August 5, 2013).

Karstadt, Myra, and Stephen Schmidt. "Olestra: Procter's Big Gamble." Center for Science in the Public Interest, March 1996. www.cspinet.org/olestra/pbg.html (accessed September 5, 2013).

Peale, Cliff. "Canadian Ban Adds to Woes for P&G's Olestra." *Cincinnati Enquirer*, June 23, 2000. www .enquirer.com/editions/2000/06/23/fin_canadian_ban_adds_to.html (accessed September 5, 2013).

A Killer Idea for Saving Lives

"Gatling Gun—Patent US0036836." United States Patent Office. patft.uspto.gov/netacgi/nph-Parser? Sect1=PTO1&Sect2=HITOFF&d=PALL&p=1&u=%2Fnetahtml%2FPTO%2Fsrchnum .htm&r=1&f=G&l=50&s1=0036836.PN.&OS=PN/0036836&RS=PN/0036836 (accessed August 6, 2013).

"Improvement in Revolving Battery-Guns: Patent US36836A." Google Patents. www.google.com/ patents/US36836 (accessed August 6, 2013).

Beyer, Rick. *The Greatest Stories Never Told: 100 Tales from History to Astonish, Bewilder, and Stupefy*. New York: HarperResource, 2003.

Wahl, Paul, and Donald R. Toppel. *The Gatling Gun*. New York: Arco Pub. Co., 1965.

The Pinhead Inventor Who Never Got the Point

Byars, Kim. "Patent for Safety Pin Issued April 10, 1849: A New Yorker Invents a Handy Device." United States Patent and Trademark Office, April 9, 2002. www.uspto.gov/news/pr/2002/02-25.jsp (accessed August 18, 2013).

Chicago Sun-Times, "Safety Pins Help Hold Our Worlds Together," February 26, 1991.

Freeman, Allyn, and Bob Golden. *Why Didn't I Think of That?: Bizarre Origins of Ingenious Inventions We Couldn't Live Without*. New York: John Wiley, 1997.

Kane, Joseph Nathan. *Necessity's Child: The Story of Walter Hunt, America's Forgotten Inventor*. Jefferson, NC: McFarland, 1997.

Wulffson, Don L., and Roy Doty. *Extraordinary Stories Behind the Invention of Ordinary Things*. New York: Lothrop, Lee and Shepard Books, 1981.

OctoBomb

Becker, Stephen. "8-Track Tapes Belong in a Museum." *NPR.org*, February 16, 2011. www.npr.org/blogs/ therecord/2011/02/17/133692586/8-track-tapes-belong-in-a-museum (accessed August 18, 2013).

Chicago Sun-Times, "Those Crazy Eights Are Back on Track," August 4, 1991.

Daley, Dan. "Audio Archeology (Eight Track Recorders)." *Tape-Disc Business*, November 1, 1999.

Hsu, Hua. "Thanks for the Memorex." *Artforum International*, February 1, 2011.

Wolf, Mark. "Cloud 8 Eight-Track Collectors Gladly Take the Bad with the Good." *Rocky Mountain News*, July 11, 2001.

Riggs, Thomas. *St. James Encyclopedia of Popular Culture*. 2nd ed. Detroit: St. James Press, 2013.

They Bet on the Ponies and Lost

"Pony Express National Historic Trail." U.S. National Park Service. www.nps.gov/poex/index.htm (accessed August 20, 2013).

"Pony Express National Historic Trail." U.S. National Park Service. www.nps.gov/poex/historyculture/index.htm (accessed August 20, 2013).

"Pony Express National Museum." Pony Express National Museum. www.ponyexpress.org/ (accessed August 20, 2013).

"Pony Express Route Map." The Caspar Collins Map Collection, Colorado State University Library. lib.colostate.edu/collins/map.html (accessed August 20, 2013).

"Pony Express Stations Across the American West." Legends of America. www.legendsofamerica.com/we-ponyexpressstations.html (accessed August 20, 2013).

Riddle, John. *The Pony Express*. Bromhal, PA: Mason Crest Publishers, 2003.

This Game Really Sticks Out in Your Mind

"Jarts." skti.org. www.skti.org/games/jarts.html (accessed August 25, 2013).

"Jarts—Death from Above!" Uncle Tom's Toys. www.uncletomstoys.com/jarts-death-from-above.html (accessed August 25, 2013).

Ferrari, Paige. "Toys Gone Bad." *Reno News Review*, May 24, 2007. www.newsreview.com/reno/toys-gone-bad/content?oid=326088 (accessed August 25, 2013).

Sawyers, Harry. "Lawn Darts." *Popular Mechanics*. www.popularmechanics.com/technology/gadgets/toys/4347051#slide-1 (accessed August 25, 2013).

A Dumb Way to Test How Smart You Are

"About Collective IQ." Doug Engelbart Institute. dougengelbart.org/about/collective-iq.html (accessed August 25, 2013).

"History of IQ Tests." Free IQ Test.net. www.free-iqtest.net/history-of-iq.asp (accessed August 25, 2013).

"Howard Gardner, Multiple Intelligences and Education." infed.org. infed.org/mobi/howard-gardner-multiple-intelligences-and-education/ (accessed August 25, 2013).

"New Book Raises Questions About IQ Test." *NPR.org*, July 3, 2007. www.npr.org/templates/story/story.php?storyId=11702932 (accessed August 25, 2013).

Connor, Steve. "IQ Tests Are 'Fundamentally Flawed' and Using Them Alone to Measure Intelligence is a 'Fallacy,' Study Finds." *Independent*, December 21, 2012. www.independent.co.uk/news/science/iq-tests-are-fundamentally-flawed-and-using-them-alone-to-measure-intelligence-is-a-fallacy-study-finds-8425911.html (accessed August 25, 2013).

Goleman, Daniel. *Emotional Intelligence*. New York: Bantam Books, 1995.

Gordon, Robert A., and Eileen E. Rudert. "Bad News Concerning IQ Tests." *American Sociological Association* 52, no. 3 (July 1979): 174-190. www.jstor.org/stable/2112323 (accessed August 25, 2013).

Murdoch, Stephen. *IQ: A Smart History of a Failed Idea*. Hoboken, NJ: J. Wiley and Sons, 2007.

Racially Insensitive Restaurant Serves Up a Side of Controversy

"Sambo's." Wikipedia. en.wikipedia.org/wiki/Sambo%27s (accessed August 25, 2013).

"The Original Sambo's Restaurant." Sambo's Restaurant. www.sambosrestaurant.com/ (accessed August 25, 2013).

LaMotte, Greg. "Sambo's Revival Running into Hot Water." *CNN.com*, January 28, 1998. www.cnn.com/US/9801/28/sambo.revival/ (accessed August 25, 2013).

New Coke's Product Launch Goes from Fizzy to Flat

"New Coke." Wikipedia. en.wikipedia.org/wiki/New_Coke (accessed August 25, 2013).

"The Real Story of New Coke." The Coca-Cola Company, November 14, 2012. www.coca-colacompany.com/stories/coke-lore-new-coke (accessed August 25, 2013).

"Top 10 Bad Beverage Ideas: New Coke." *TIME.com*. www.time.com/time/specials/packages/article/0,28804,1913612_1913610_1913608,00.html (accessed August 25, 2013).

Ross, Michael E. "It Seemed Like a Good Idea at the Time: New Coke, 20 Years Later, and Other Marketing Fiascoes." *NBCNews.com*, April 22, 2005. www.nbcnews.com/id/7209828/ns/us_news/t/it-seemed-good-idea-time/#.UhnDdtJzGSo (accessed August 25, 2013).

The Pubic Hairpiece

"Merkin." Uncyclopedia. uncyclopedia.wikia.com/wiki/Merkin (accessed August 26, 2013).

"Merkin." Urban Dictionary. www.urbandictionary.com/define.php?term=merkin (accessed August 26, 2013).

"Merkin." Wikipedia. en.wikipedia.org/wiki/Merkin (accessed August 26, 2013).

Francis, Gareth. "A Short and Curly History of the Merkin." *Guardian*, June 26, 2003. www.theguardian.com/theguardian/2003/jun/26/features11.g2 (accessed August 26, 2013).

WD-528,000,000,000

"About Us." WD-40.com. wd40.com/about-us/history/ (accessed August 29, 2013).

Bellis, Mary. "WD-40." About.com. inventors.about.com/od/wstartinventions/a/WDFourty.htm (accessed August 29, 2013).

Monkey Business Sinks a Presidential Campaign

Gray, Madison, and S. James Snyder. "Top 10 Political Sex Scandals: Gary Hart." *TIME.com*, June 8, 2011. www.time.com/time/specials/2007/article/0,28804,1721111_1721210_1721112,00.html (accessed August 6, 2013).

McGee, Jim, Tom Fiedler, and James Savage. "The Gary Hart Story: How It Happened." *Miami Herald*, May 10, 1987. www.unc.edu/%7Epmeyer/Hart/hartarticle.html (accessed August 6, 2013).

Ross, Shelley. *Fall From Grace: Sex, Scandal, and Corruption in American Politics from 1702 to the Present.* New York: Ballantine Books, 1988.

Thompson, John B. *Political Scandal: Power and Visibility in the Media Age.* Cambridge: Polity Press, 2000.

Tape Creates a Sticky Situation for Tricky Dick

"A Chance to Fill in the Gap; Experts May Try to Recover Watergate Tape's 18 1/2 Minutes." *Washington Post*, August 22, 2000.

Bernstein, Carl, and Bob Woodward. *All the President's Men*. New York: Simon and Schuster, 1974.

Fisher, Marc. "Watergate at 40." *Washington Post*, June 14, 2012. www.washingtonpost.com/watergate (accessed August 17, 2013).

Woodward, Bob, and Carl Bernstein. *The Secret Man: the story of Watergate's Deep Throat*. New York: Simon & Schuster, 2005.

Maguire, Ken. "Former Nixon Aide Says History Was Motivation for Oval Office Recordings." *AP Worldstream*, February 17, 2003.

The Grand High Exalted Hoo-Hah of the United States

Edwards, Ben. "Idea Starter: Selecting a Title for the President." Teach History. teachhistory.com/tag/john-adams (accessed August 21, 2013).

Hart, Albert Bushnell. *Formation of the Union, 1750-1829*. 8th ed. New York: Longmans, Green, 1897.

Wood, Gordon S. *The Radicalism of the American Revolution*. New York: A. A. Knopf, 1992.

A Turkey of an Idea Gets Plucked

Beyer, Rick. *The Greatest Stories Never Told: 100 Tales from History to Astonish, Bewilder, and Stupefy*. New York: HarperResource, 2003.

Rosenberg, Jennifer. "How FDR Changed Thanksgiving." About.com. history1900s.about.com/od/1930s/a/thanksgiving.htm (accessed August 21, 2013).

Soniak, Matt. "Happy Franksgiving: Why FDR Rescheduled Turkey Day." *Mental Floss*. mentalfloss.com/article/29317/happy-franksgiving-why-fdr-rescheduled-turkey-day (accessed August 21, 2013).

Zorn, Eric. "7 Good Reasons to Reschedule Thanksgiving." *Chicago Tribune*, November 25, 2005. articles.chicagotribune.com/2005-11-25/news/0511250223_1_thanksgiving-day-pilgrim-indian-heavy-snow (accessed August 21, 2013).

Mail to the Chief

"Zachary Taylor." United States History. www.u-s-history.com/pages/h132.html (accessed August 25, 2013).

Eisenhower, John S. D. *Zachary Taylor*. New York: Times Books, 2008.

Freidel, Frank, and Hugh Sidey. "Zachary Taylor." The White House. www.whitehouse.gov/about/presidents/zacharytaylor/ (accessed August 25, 2013).

The Bridge to Nowhere

"$315 Million Bridge to Nowhere." Taxpayer.net, February 9, 2005. www.taxpayer.net/user_uploads/file/Transportation/gravinabridge.pdf (accessed August 25, 2013).

"Alaska: End Sought for 'Bridge to Nowhere.'" *New York Times*, September 22, 2007. query.nytimes.com/gst/fullpage.html?res=9A04E7D81F3AF931A1575AC0A9619C8B63 (accessed August 26, 2013).

Grunwald, Michael. "Pork by Any Other Name…" *Washington Post*, April 30, 2006. www.washingtonpost
.com/wp-dyn/content/article/2006/04/29/AR2006042900141.html (accessed August 25, 2013).

Utt, Ronald D., Ph.D. "The Bridge to Nowhere: A National Embarrassment." The Heritage Foundation.
www.heritage.org/research/reports/2005/10/the-bridge-to-nowhere-a-national-
embarrassment (accessed August 26, 2013).

Make Your Meeting or Else Meet Your Maker

Beyer, Rick. *The Greatest Presidential Stories Never Told: 100 Tales from History to Astonish, Bewilder, and
Stupefy*. New York: Collins, 2007.

Lammle, Rob. "A Brief History of Bulletproof Vests." *Mental Floss*. mentalfloss.com/article/24039/brief-
history-bulletproof-vests (accessed August 6, 2013).

For Whom the City of Bell Tolls

"Retrial in Bell Corruption Case Unlikely Until Early 2014." *CBSLA.com*, May 29, 2013. losangeles
.cbslocal.com/2013/05/29/retrial-in-bell-corruption-case-unlikely-until-early-2014/
(accessed August 26, 2013).

"The Devil Bell Knows." *Los Angeles Times*, September 2, 2010. www.latimes.com/news/opinion/
editorials/la-ed-bell-20100902,0,1549951.story (accessed August 26, 2013).

Coolican, J. Patrick. "City of Bell Corruption: The People Yell over the Smell in the Hell That is Bell."
LA Weekly, July 29, 2010. www.laweekly.com/2010-07-29/news/city-of-bell-corruption/
(accessed August 26, 2013).

Schuker, Lauren A. E. "High Salaries of City's Administrators Spur Resignations." *Wall Street Journal*, July
23, 2010. online.wsj.com/article/SB10001424052748704249004575385500597789846.html
(accessed August 26, 2013).

Welch, William M. "5 of 6 Officials Guilty in Bell, Calif., Corruption Case." *USATODAY.com*, March
21, 2013. www.usatoday.com/story/news/nation/2013/03/20/bell-corruption-conviction-
california/2003473/ (accessed August 26, 2013).

The President Gives America the Finger

"A Chronology: Key Moments in the Clinton-Lewinsky Saga." *CNN.com*. www.cnn.com/
ALLPOLITICS/1998/resources/lewinsky/timeline/ (accessed August 26, 2013).

"Did He Just Say That? Bill Clinton." *TIME.com*. www.time.com/time/specials/packages/
article/0,28804,1859513_1859526_1859515,00.html (accessed August 26, 2013).

"Lewinsky Scandal." Answers.com. www.answers.com/topic/lewinsky-scandal (accessed August 26, 2013).

"The Stained Blue Dress that Almost Lost a Presidency." University of Missouri-Kansas City School of Law.
law2.umkc.edu/faculty/projects/ftrials/clinton/lewinskydress.html (accessed August 26, 2013).

Baker, Peter, and John F. Harris. "Clinton Admits to Lewinsky Relationship, Challenges Starr to End
Personal 'Prying.'" *Washington Post*, August 18, 1998. www.washingtonpost.com/wp-srv/
politics/special/clinton/stories/clinton081898.htm (accessed August 26, 2013).

Miller, Jake. "15 Years Ago: Bill Clinton's Historic Denial." *CBSNews.com*, January 25, 2013. www
.cbsnews.com/8301-250_162-57565928/15-years-ago-bill-clintons-historic-denial/ (accessed
August 26, 2013).

Nelson, Steven. "I Did Not Have Sexual Relations with That Woman: Bill Clinton 15 Years Ago." *U.S.
News & World Report*. www.usnews.com/news/blogs/press-past/2013/01/25/bill-clinton-15-
years-ago-i-did-not-have-sexual-relations-with-that-woman (accessed August 26, 2013).

Posner, Richard A. *An Affair of State: The Investigation, Impeachment, and Trial of President Clinton*.
Cambridge, MA: Harvard University Press, 1999.

Read My Lips: No New Taxes (Until I Change My Mind)

"Did He Just Say That? George H.W. Bush." *TIME.com*. www.time.com/time/specials/packages/
article/0,28804,1859513_1859526_1859516,00.html (accessed August 30, 2013).

Ellis, Ryan. "'Read My Lips' Won't Happen Again." *National Review Online*, June 13, 2011. www
.nationalreview.com/articles/269397/read-my-lips-won-t-happen-again-ryan-ellis (accessed
August 30, 2013).

Kessler, Glenn. "Grover Norquist's History Lesson: George H. W. Bush, 'No New Taxes,' and the 1992 Election."
Washington Post, November 27, 2012. www.washingtonpost.com/blogs/fact-checker/post/grover-
norquists-history-lesson-george-hw-bush-no-new-taxes-and-the-1992-election/2012/11/26/
cfd6d65a-3811-11e2-8a97-363b0f9a0ab3_blog.html (accessed August 30, 2013).

Pay No Attention to That Exploding Mountain—Just Vote for Me

"May 7, 1902: Volcanic Eruption Buries Caribbean City." History.com. www.history.com/this-day-in-
history/volcanic-eruption-buries-caribbean-city (accessed August 30, 2013).

"Unknown History: Election Day Deaths." History Confidential, March 3, 2009. www.historyconfidential
.com/2009/03/unknown-history-election-day-deaths/ (accessed August 30, 2013).

Fisher, Richard V., Grant Heiken, and Jeffrey B. Hulen. "Politicians and Volcanoes." Chap. 1 in *Volcanoes:
Crucibles of Change*. Princeton, NJ: Princeton University Press, 1997.

Pol Pays a Hooker by Check and Really Gets Screwed

"Jerry Springer." Wikipedia. en.wikipedia.org/?title=Jerry_Springer (accessed August 30, 2013).

Gray, Madison, and S. James Snyder. "Top 10 Political Sex Scandals: Jerry Springer." *TIME.com*, June 8,
2011. content.time.com/time/specials/2007/article/0,28804,1721111_1721210_1721110,00
.html (accessed August 30, 2013).

This Is How I Look—and I'm Not Making It Up

"The Kennedy-Nixon Debates." History.com. www.history.com/topics/kennedy-nixon-debates
(accessed September 1, 2013).

Beyer, Rick. *The Greatest Presidential Stories Never Told: 100 Tales from History to Astonish, Bewilder, and
Stupefy*. New York: Collins, 2007.

Schroeder, Alan. *Presidential Debates: Forty Years of High-risk TV*. New York: Columbia University Press, 2000.

Webley, Kayla. "How the Nixon-Kennedy Debate Changed the World." *TIME.com*, September 23, 2010.
content.time.com/time/nation/article/0,8599,2021078,00.html (accessed September 1, 2013).

Ten of the Worst Movie Ideas in History

Medved, Harry, and Randy Dreyfuss. *The Fifty Worst Films of All Time (And How They Got That Way)*. New York: Popular Library, 1978.

Medved, Harry, and Michael Medved. *The Golden Turkey Awards: The Worst Achievements in Hollywood History*. New York: Putnam, 1980.

———. *Son of Golden Turkey Awards*. New York: Villard Books, 1986.

Noah, Timothy. "Valley of the Duds; Inside Hollywood's Bad Movie Machine." *Washington Monthly*, October 1, 1985.

Wilson, John. *The Official Razzie Movie Guide: Enjoying the Best of Hollywood's Worst*. New York: Warner Books, 2005.

The Bambino's Curse on the Beantown Bombers

The Curse of the Bambino. DVD. Directed by George Roy. New York: Home Box Office, 2003.

Corcoran, Cliff. "99 Cool Facts about Babe Ruth." *Sports Illustrated*, July 14, 2013. mlb.si.com/2013/07/11/99-cool-facts-about-babe-ruth/ (accessed August 6, 2013).

Wann, Daniel L., and Len Zaichkowsky. "Sport Team Identification and Belief in Team Curses: The Case of the Boston Red Sox and the Curse of the Bambino." *Journal of Sport Behavior*, December 1, 2009.

Fourth Down and 70 Million to Go

Farhi, Paul. "XFL's Strategy: First and Twenty-Something." *Washington Post*, February 3, 2001.

Forrest, Brett. *Long Bomb: How the XFL Became TV's Biggest Fiasco*. New York: Crown Publishers, 2002.

Rushin, Steve. "Dumbest Sports Moments." *Sports Illustrated*, September 27, 2004. sportsillustrated.cnn.com/vault/article/magazine/MAG1103781/2/index.htm (accessed August 17, 2013).

Washington Post. "The XFL, Not as Bad as It Wanted to Be." May 12, 2001.

The Heavyweight Chomping-On of the World

"Evander Holyfield Retains Title; Mike Tyson Disqualified for Biting." *Jet*, July 14, 1997.

Rushin, Steve. "Dumbest Sports Moments." *Sports Illustrated*, September 27, 2004. sportsillustrated.cnn.com/vault/article/magazine/MAG1103781/ (accessed August 20, 2013).

Washington Post. "Bizarre End to Rematch of Title Bout; Holyfield Keeps Crown after Two Tyson Bites," June 29, 1997.

Washington Post. "The Ear Marks of a Champion; Since Tyson's Bloody Bite, Holyfield Is a 'Bigger Hero' to Many Fans." November 7, 1997.

Willis, George. *The Bite Fight: Tyson, Holyfield, and the Night That Changed Boxing Forever*. Chicago: Triumph Books LLC, 2013.

Out of the Park? Out of the Question

"A Catch Worthy of Jackie Robinson; Library of Congress Snags the Papers of African American Baseball Great." *Washington Post*, November 6, 2001.

"Giving the Past a Future: Exhibit in Washington Pays Tribute to Negro Leagues Slugger Josh Gibson." *Baltimore Sun*, June 7, 2007.

"Josh Gibson." Baseball-Reference.com. www.baseball-reference.com/bullpen/Josh_Gibson (accessed August 20, 2013).

Schwartz, Larry. "No Joshing About Gibson's Talents." *ESPN.com.* espn.go.com/sportscentury/features/00016050 .html (accessed August 20, 2013).

Dopey Cyclist Pedals a Pack of Lies

"Cyclist Floyd Landis Reaches Deal on Fraud Counts." *CBSNews.com*, August 24, 2012. www.cbsnews .com/8301-400_162-57499580/cyclist-floyd-landis-reaches-deal-on-fraud-counts/ (accessed August 25, 2013).

Clarke, Liz. "Floyd Landis Whistleblower Suit Targets More Than Lance Armstrong." *Washington Post*, January 17, 2013. articles.washingtonpost.com/2013-01-17/sports/36409945_1_tour-de-france-titles-whistleblower-suit-floyd-landis (accessed August 25, 2013).

Dreier, Frederick. "Floyd Landis Calls Pro Cycling 'Organized Crime.'" *USA TODAY*, February 13, 2013. www.usatoday.com/story/sports/cycling/2013/02/13/floyd-landis-pro-cycling-is-organized-crime/1916805/ (accessed August 25, 2013).

Dreier, Frederick. "Floyd Landis: Cycling Body was Complicit in Doping." *USA TODAY*, February 28, 2013. www.usatoday.com/story/sports/cycling/2013/02/28/doping-cycling-floyd-landis-travis-tygart/1954969/ (accessed August 25, 2013).

Hosenball, Mark. "Why Landis Went After Lance." *Newsweek*, August 7, 2010. www.thedailybeast.com/ newsweek/2010/08/07/roots-of-a-rift.html (accessed August 25, 2013).

Macur, Juliet, and Michael Schmidt. "Landis Admits Doping, Accuses Top U.S. Cyclists." *New York Times*, May 20, 2010. www.nytimes.com/2010/05/21/sports/cycling/21landis .html?ref=floydlandis&_r=0 (accessed August 25, 2013).

A Multimillion-Dollar Career Goes to the Dogs

"Michael Vick." *FOXSports.com.* msn.foxsports.com/nfl/player/michael-vick/69083?q=michael-vick (accessed August 26, 2013).

Maske, Mark. "Falcons' Vick Indicted in Dogfighting Case." *Washington Post*, July 18, 2007. www .washingtonpost.com/wp-dyn/content/article/2007/07/17/AR2007071701393.html (accessed August 26, 2013).

Schmidt, Michael S. "Vick Pleads Guilty in Dog-Fighting Case." *New York Times*, August 27, 2007. www .nytimes.com/2007/08/27/sports/football/27cnd-vick.html?_r=0 (accessed August 26, 2013).

Disco Inferno Singes the White Sox

Behrens, Andy. "Disco Demolition: Bell-Bottoms Be Gone!" *ESPN.com*, July 12, 2009. sports.espn .go.com/espn/page3/story?page=behrens/040809 (accessed August 29, 2013).

Graves, Jeremiah. "30 Years Later: Disco Demolition Night." Bleacher Report, July 12, 2009. bleacherreport .com/articles/216590-30-years-later-disco-demolition-night (accessed August 29, 2013).

LaPointe, Joe. "The Night Disco Went Up in Smoke." *New York Times*, July 4, 2009. www.nytimes .com/2009/07/05/sports/baseball/05disco.html (accessed August 29, 2013).

Not a Guy You Want to Neck With

"Christie Prody Injured; O. J. Simpson Not a Suspect." *Hollywood Gossip*, February 13, 2008. www .thehollywoodgossip.com/2008/02/christie-prody-injured-oj-simpson-not-a-suspect/ (accessed August 31, 2013).

"Christine Prody is O. J. Simpson's Girlfriend." Right Fielders, September 18, 2007. sports.rightpundits .com/?p=210 (accessed August 31, 2013).

"O. J. Simpson Ex-Girlfriend's Shocking Tell-All." *National Enquirer*, April 14, 2009. www .nationalenquirer.com/crime-investigation/oj-simpson-ex-girlfriends-shocking-tell-all (accessed August 31, 2013).

"O. J. Simpson's Girlfriend Does Not Want Him Released From Jail." Radar Online, August 4, 2009. radaronline.com/exclusives/2009/08/exclusive-oj-simpsons-girlfriend-does-not-want-him-released-jail/ (accessed August 31, 2013).

Landman, Beth, and Anne Adams Lang. "When the Homicidal Maniac's Away…" *New York Magazine*, November 13, 1995. books.google.com/books?id=beQCAAAAMBAJ&pg=PA24#v=onepage&q&f=false (accessed August 31, 2013).

We Qaeda Sorta Attacked the Wrong Country

"9/11 by the Numbers." *New York Magazine*. nymag.com/news/articles/wtc/1year/numbers.htm (accessed August 19, 2013).

"2003 Invasion of Iraq." WordIQ.com. www.wordiq.com/definition/2003_invasion_of_Iraq (accessed August 19, 2013).

"Explain Again Why We Invaded Iraq?" *Baltimore Sun*, January 4, 2012. articles.baltimoresun.com/2012-01-04/news/bs-ed-iraq-invasion-letter-20120104_1_chemical-weapons-iraq-saddam-hussein (accessed August 19, 2013).

"The Invasion of Iraq." *PBS.org*. www.pbs.org/wgbh/pages/frontline/shows/invasion/ (accessed August 19, 2013).

Lind, Michael. "How Neoconservatives Conquered Washington—and Launched a War." Antiwar.com, April 19, 2003. www.antiwar.com/orig/lind1.html (accessed August 19, 2013).

Shah, Anup. "Iraq: 2003 onwards; War, Aftermath and Post-Saddam." Global Issues, December 12, 2010. www.globalissues.org/article/423/iraq-2003-onwards-war-aftermath-and-post-saddam (accessed August 19, 2013).

A Single Torpedo Sinks the German Ship of State

"The Sinking of the *Lusitania*." EyeWitness to History.com. www.eyewitnesstohistory.com/snpwwi2 .htm (accessed August 21, 2013).

Greenhill, Sam. "Secret of the *Lusitania*: Arms Find Challenges Allied Claims It Was Solely a Passenger Ship." *Daily Mail Online*, December 20, 2008. www.dailymail.co.uk/news/article-1098904/ Secret-Lusitania-Arms-challenges-Allied-claims-solely-passenger-ship.html (accessed August 21, 2013).

Hickey, Des, and Gus Smith. *Seven Days to Disaster: The Sinking of the* Lusitania. New York: Putnam, 1981.

Jones, Nigel. "Was the *Lusitania* Britain's War Crime? 1,198 Passengers Died in 1915 When the Liner
Sank—but Was a German Torpedo Really to Blame?" *London Daily Mail*, July 13, 2012.

Rosenberg, Jennifer. "Sinking of the *Lusitania*." About.com. history1900s.about.com/cs/worldwari/p/
lusitania.htm (accessed August 21, 2013).

Simpson, Colin. *The Lusitania*. 1st American ed. Boston: Little, Brown, 1973.

The Double Agent Who Double-Crossed der Führer

"Operation Fortitude." Wikipedia. en.wikipedia.org/wiki/Operation_Fortitude (accessed August 25, 2013).

Isby, David C. "World War II: Double Agent's D-Day Victory." History Net.com, June 12, 2006. www
.historynet.com/world-war-ii-double-agents-d-day-victory.htm (accessed August 25, 2013).

Polmar, Norman, and Thomas B. Allen. "Spy Fact of the Day: Garbo." Random House. www
.randomhouse.com/features/spybook/spy/961204.html (accessed August 25, 2013).

Invade Russia in the Winter? Snow Way!

"Operation Barbarossa." Wikipedia. en.wikipedia.org/wiki/Operation_Barbarossa (accessed August 29, 2013).

McDonald, Jason. "The Invasion of Russia June 22, 1941–December 1941." The World War II
Multimedia Database, July 25, 2011. worldwar2database.com/html/barbarossa.htm (accessed
August 29, 2013).

Rees, Laurence. *War of the Century: When Hitler Fought Stalin*. New York: New Press, 1999.

Rees, Laurence. "Hitler's Invasion of Russia in World War Two." BBC History, March 30, 2011. www
.bbc.co.uk/history/worldwars/wwtwo/hitler_russia_invasion_01.shtml (accessed August 26, 2013).

The Boston Globe. "Operation Barbarossa." February 11, 2004.

A Military Strategy That's Dead On

Burr, William. "The Atomic Bomb and the End of World War II." The National Security Archive, April 27,
2007. www2.gwu.edu/~nsarchiv/NSAEBB/NSAEBB162/index.htm (accessed August 30, 2013).

Onoda, Hiroo. *No Surrender: My Thirty-Year War*. Tokyo: Kodansha International, 1974.

Powers, David. "Japan: No Surrender in World War Two." BBC History, February 17, 2011. www.bbc
.co.uk/history/worldwars/wwtwo/japan_no_surrender_01.shtml (accessed August 30, 2013).

You Better Watch Out, You Better Not Cry, You Better Read Your Mail, I'm Telling You Why: Sneaky George Is Coming to Town

"George Washington's Crossing of the Delaware River." Wikipedia. en.wikipedia.org/wiki/
Washington%27s_crossing_of_the_Delaware (accessed August 31, 2013).

"Washington's Surprise Attack on Trenton." History.com. www.history.com/videos/george-washington-
makes-surprise-attack-on-trenton#jefferson-writes-the-declaration-of-independence
(accessed August 31, 2013).

Fischer, David Hackett. *Washington's Crossing*. Oxford: Oxford University Press, 2004.

Lass, Cody. "Battle of Trenton (December 26, 1776)." George Washington's Mount Vernon. www
.mountvernon.org/educational-resources/encyclopedia/battle-trenton (accessed August 31, 2013).

Moran, Donald N. "Colonel Johann Gottlieb Rall: Guilty of Tactical Negligence or Guiltless Circumstances?" Sons of the American Revolution. www.revolutionarywararchives.org/rall. html (accessed August 31, 2013).

Caesar's Fiery Battle Tactics Leave Historians Burning Mad

"Library of Alexandria." Crystalinks.com. www.crystalinks.com/libraryofalexandria.html (accessed August 31, 2013).

"The Lost Books of the Bible." The Bible UFO Connection. www.bibleufo.com/anomlostbooks1.htm (accessed August 31, 2013).

"The Missing Books Mentioned in the Bible." DocStoc.com. www.docstoc.com/docs/9519193/The-Missing-Books-Mentioned-In-The-Bible (accessed August 30, 2013).

Chesser, Preston. "The Burning of the Library of Alexandria." eHistory Archive. ehistory.osu.edu/world/articles/ArticleView.cfm?AID=9 (accessed August 31, 2013).

Hannam, James. "The Mysterious Fate of the Great Library of Alexandria." Bede's Library. www.bede.org.uk/library.htm (accessed August 31, 2013).

Kelly, Stuart. "The Missing Masterpieces." *London Independent*, August 19, 2005. www.independent.co.uk/arts entertainment/books/features/the-missing-masterpieces-6143584.html (accessed August 31, 2013).

America's Best General Gets a Slap in the Face

"On This Day: George S. Patton Slaps Hospitalized Soldier." findingDulcinea, August 3, 2011. www.findingdulcinea.com/news/on-this-day/July-August-08/On-this-Day-General-Patton-Shocks-Public-by-Slapping-Crying-Soldier.html (accessed September 1, 2013).

Patton. Film. Directed by Franklin J. Schaffner. Beverly Hills, CA: 20th Century Fox Home Entertainment, 2006.

D'Este, Carlo. "The Triumph and Tragedy of George S. Patton, Jr.: The Slapping Incidents in Sicily." ArmchairGeneral.com, May 4, 2005. www.armchairgeneral.com/the-triumph-and-tragedy-of-george-s-patton-jr-the-slapping-incidents-in-sicily.htm (accessed August 31, 2013).

Fashion Frock-Ups: Pick Your Favorite Worst Ideas for Under-, Outer-, Foot-, and Headwear

"Cage Crinoline." The Metropolitan Museum of Art. metmuseum.org/collections/search-the-collections/157055 (accessed August 18, 2013).

Goldberg, Michael Jay. *The Collectible '70s A Price Guide to the Polyester Decade*. Cincinnati: F+W Media, 2011.

Long, Mark A., and Jim Fee. *Bad Fads*. Toronto: ECW Press, 2002.

Meadows, Celia, and Leslie Stall Widener. *Why Would Anyone Wear That?: Fascinating Fashion Facts*. New York: Intellect, 2012.

Thomas, Pauline Weston. "Crinolines Fashion History." Fashion-Era.com. www.fashion-era.com/crinolines.htm (accessed August 18, 2013).

Hats Off to the World's Maddest Profession

"Mad as a Hatter." Corrosion Doctors. www.corrosion-doctors.org/Elements-Toxic/Mercury-mad-hatter.htm (accessed August 5, 2013).

"Mercury Poisoning." Infoplease.com. www.infoplease.com/ce6/sci/A0832760.html (accessed August 5, 2013).

Itri, Patricia Ward, and Frank M. Itri. *Mercury Contamination: A Human Tragedy*. New York: Wiley, 1977.

Waldron, H. A. "Did the Mad Hatter Have Mercury Poisoning?" *British Medical Journal* 287, no. 6409 (December 24, 1983): 1961. www.ncbi.nlm.nih.gov/pmc/articles/PMC1550196/ (accessed August 5, 2013).

Help Yourself to a Steaming Cup of Influenza

Crosby, Alfred W. *America's Forgotten Pandemic: The Influenza of 1918*. 2nd ed. Cambridge: Cambridge University Press, 2003.

Getz, David, and Peter McCarty. *Purple Death: The Mysterious Flu of 1918*. New York: Henry Holt, 2000.

Kolata, Gina Bari. *Flu: The Story of the Great Influenza Pandemic of 1918 and the Search for the Virus That Caused It*. New York: Farrar, Straus and Giroux, 1999.

Webster, Robert G. "A Molecular Whodunit." *Science* 293, no. 5536 (September 7, 2001): 1773-1775.

A Dental Care Product That Could Rot Your Teeth

Washington Post. "It's the Real Thing—or Is It?; Georgia Man Says He Has Coca-Cola's Original Recipe." October 5, 1996.

"The Recipe." This American Life. www.thisamericanlife.org/radio-archives/episode/427/original-recipe/recipe (accessed August 21, 2013).

Pendergrast, Mark. *For God, Country, and Coca-Cola*. New York: Scribner's, 1993.

The Coca-Cola Company. "Coca-Cola Heritage Timeline." Coca-Cola History. heritage.coca-cola.com/ (accessed August 20, 2013).

Lincoln's Mercury Dealers Nearly Drive the President Crazy

"Mercury in Anti-Depressant Medication Could Have Caused Abraham Lincoln's Bad-Tempered Outbursts." *History Today*, September 1, 2001.

Davis, Jeanie Lerche. "Lincoln's Little Blue Pills." WebMD.com, July 17, 2001. www.webmd.com/depression/news/20010717/lincolns-little-blue-pills (accessed August 29, 2013).

Shenk, Joshua Wolf. "Lincoln's Great Depression." *Atlantic*, October 1, 2005. www.theatlantic.com/magazine/archive/2005/10/lincoln-apos-s-great-depression/4247/ (accessed August 29, 2013).

Shenk, Joshua Wolf. *Lincoln's Melancholy: How Depression Challenged a President and Fueled His Greatness*. Boston: Houghton Mifflin Co., 2005.

The Hippocratic Cure Only Dracula Could Love

"Blood, Bandages, and Barber Poles." h2g2.com, November 29, 2002. h2g2.com/dna/h2g2/brunel/A885062 (accessed August 21, 2013).

"Bloodletting." Answers.com. www.answers.com/topic/bloodletting (accessed August 17, 2013).

"Bloodletting." London Science Museum. www.sciencemuseum.org.uk/broughttolife/techniques/bloodletting.aspx (accessed August 21, 2013).

Seigworth, Gilbert R. "A Brief History of Bloodletting." *PBS.org*. www.pbs.org/wnet/redgold/basics/bloodlettinghistory.html (accessed August 21, 2013).

Ignorance Is Dr. Bliss

"How Alexander Graham Bell Helped Kill the President." EinsteinsRefrigerator.com. einsteinsrefrigerator.com/garfield/ (accessed August 25, 2013).

Beyer, Rick. *The Greatest Presidential Stories Never Told: 100 Tales from History to Astonish, Bewilder, and Stupefy*. New York: Collins, 2007.

Panati, Charles. *Panati's Extraordinary Endings of Practically Everything and Everybody*. New York: Perennial Library, 1989.

Rasmussen, Frederick N. "Medical Bungling Most Likely Killed Garfield." *Baltimore Sun*, October 15, 2011. articles.baltimoresun.com/2011-10-15/news/bs-md-backstory-garfield-continued-20111015_1_garfield-surgery-baltimore-potomac-railroad (accessed August 25, 2013).

The Dental Amalgam That Might Have You Feeling Down in the Mouth

"Dental Amalgam Mercury Fillings." Dental Amalgam Mercury Solutions. amalgam.org/ (accessed August 25, 2013).

Braunstein, Michael. "Mercury Fillings: Just Say 'Nahhhh.'" Heartland Healing Center. www.heartlandhealing.com/pages/reader/mercury_fillings.html (accessed August 26, 2013).

Kaupi, Monica. "Amalgam Can Cause Brain Damage in Children." Heavy Metal Bulletin. www.holisticmed.com/dental/amalgam/child.html (accessed August 26, 2013).

Oz, Mehmet. "Toxic Teeth: Are Mercury Fillings Making You Sick?" The Dr. Oz Show. www.doctoroz.com/videos/toxic-teeth-are-mercury-fillings-making-you-sick-pt-1 (accessed August 26, 2013).

Balloon Boy Floats a Story Full of Hot Air

Chandrashekhar, Vaishnavi. "Goal of Guilty Plea in Balloon Boy Case: Mom Won't Be Deported." *Christian Science Monitor*, November 12, 2009.

Seattle Post-Intelligencer. "Affidavit: Heene Parents 'Knew All Along' Son Wasn't in Balloon." October 24, 2009.

Seattle Post-Intelligencer. "Richard Heene Reports to Jail." January 11, 2010.

Sappenfield, Mark. "Colorado Went to Huge Lengths to Save Balloon Boy Falcon Heene." *Christian Science Monitor*, October 15, 2009.

India's Roll of the Dice Comes Up an Unlucky "Sevin"

"Frequently Asked Questions Regarding the Bhopal Tragedy of 1984." Bhopal Information Center, November 2010. www.bhopal.com/faq#faq1 (accessed August 29, 2013).

"The Incident, Response, and Settlement." Bhopal Information Center. www.bhopal.com/incident-response-and-settlement (accessed August 29, 2013).

Broughton, Edward. "The Bhopal Disaster and Its Aftermath." *Environmental Health* 4, no. 6 (2005). www.ehjournal.net/content/4/1/6 (accessed August 29, 2013).

Tully, Mark. "US Firm 'Knew of Dangers' at Bhopal Plant." *BBC News*, December 2, 2004. news.bbc .co.uk/2/hi/programmes/file_on_4/4062611.stm (accessed August 29, 2013).

Eight Is More Than Enough

"A Conversation with Nadya Suleman." Oprah.com. www.oprah.com/oprahshow/Oprah-Interviews-Nadya-Suleman (accessed August 29, 2013).

"Nadya Suleman's Reality Series Is Official." *Boston Herald*, June 1, 2009. bostonherald.com/inside_track/star_ tracks/2009/06/nadya_suleman%E2%80%99s_reality_series_official (accessed August 29, 2013).

"Octomom." *TMZ.com.* www.tmz.com/person/octomom/ (accessed August 29, 2013).

"'Octomom' Nadya Suleman Faces Eviction this Week." *Los Angeles Times*, March 27, 2012. latimesblogs .latimes.com/lanow/2012/03/octomom-nadya-suleman-faces-eviction-this-week-.html (accessed August 29, 2013).

"'Octomom' Nadya Suleman Reportedly Auctioning Date Online." *Los Angeles Times*, August 6, 2012. latimesblogs.latimes.com/lanow/2012/08/octomom-nadya-suleman-reportedly-auctioning-date-online.html (accessed August 29, 2013).

"'Octomom' Nadya Suleman's Doctor Wants His Medical License Back." *Los Angeles Times*, November 23, 2011. latimesblogs.latimes.com/lanow/2011/11/octomom-nadya-suleman-michael-kamrava-doctor-license-octuplets.html (accessed August 29, 2013).

Ponsi, Lou. "'Octomom' Nadya Suleman Files Bankruptcy Papers." *Boston Herald*, May 1, 2012. bostonherald. com/inside_track/celebrity_news/2012/05/%E2%80%98octomom%E2%80%99_nadya_ suleman_files_bankruptcy_papers (accessed August 29, 2013).

Y2K Is A-OK

"Y2K Bug." Encyclopedia Britannica. www.britannica.com/EBchecked/topic/382740/Y2K-bug (accessed August 18, 2013).

Asher, Joe. "Y2K: Keep Sending That Message." *ABA Banking Journal*, September 1, 1999.

Bullers, Finn. "Y2K Doomsayer Now Thinks the Result Will Be Only a Six-Month Recession." *Knight Ridder/Tribune Business News*, November 11, 1999.

Farrell, Chris, Ochen Kaylan, and Catherine Winter. "The Surprising Legacy of Y2K." American RadioWorks. americanradioworks.publicradio.org/features/y2k/ (accessed August 18, 2013).

Murray, Jerome T., and Marilyn J. Murray. *Computers in Crisis: How to Avert the Coming Worldwide Computer Systems Collapse*. New York: PBI, 1984.

The London Big Mac Smackdown

"McLibel." IMDb. www.imdb.com/title/tt0458425/ (accessed August 20, 2013).

"McLibel: British Activists Sued for Distributing McDonald's: Flyers Win Court Case." Democracy Now! www.democracynow.org/2005/2/16/mclibel_british_activists_sued_for_distributing (accessed August 20, 2013).

"McLibel case." Wikipedia. en.wikipedia.org/wiki/McLibel_case (accessed August 20, 2013).

"McLibel: Longest case in English history." *BBC News*, February 15, 2005. news.bbc.co.uk/2/hi/uk_ news/4266741.stm (accessed August 20, 2013).

Byrne, Caroline. "Scotland Yard Settles McLibel Case." *AP News Archive*, July 5, 2000. www.apnewsarchive .com/2000/Scotland-Yard-Settles-McLibel-Case/id-8cfa1fccd21f488635607a353133bae7 (accessed August 17, 2013).

Cattlemen's Beef with Oprah Needs More Cowbell

"Oprah Accused of Whipping Up Anti-Beef 'Lynch Mob.'" *CNN.com*, January 21, 1998. www.cnn .com/US/9801/21/oprah.beef/ (accessed August 29, 2013).

"Oprah Winfrey vs. the Beef People." *PBS NewsHour*, January 20, 1998. www.pbs.org/newshour/bb/ law/jan-june98/fooddef_1-20.html (accessed August 29, 2013).

Silverman, Stephen M. "Judge Puts Beef Against Oprah to Rest." *People.com*, September 18, 2002. www .people.com/people/article/0,,624749,00.html (accessed August 29, 2013).

Stephey, M. J. "Where's the Beef?" *TIME.com*, May 25, 2011. content.time.com/time/specials/packages/ article/0,28804,1939460_1939452_1939475,00.html (accessed August 29, 2013).

Bernie Made-Off with Their Money

Lenzner, Robert. "Bernie Madoff's $50 Billion Ponzi Scheme." *Forbes*, December 12, 2008. www.forbes .com/2008/12/12/madoff-ponzi-hedge-pf-ii-in_rl_1212croesus_inl.html (accessed August 6, 2013).

The New York Times. "A Timeline of the Madoff Fraud - Interactive Feature." NYTimes.com. www .nytimes.com/interactive/2009/06/29/business/madoff-timeline.html (accessed August 6, 2013).

Break Glass and Get Thirty Years of Bad Luck

Browne, Clayton. "Regulation vs Deregulation: Laissez-Faire or Regulate?" Suite 101, June 27, 2010. suite101.com/article/economic-regulation-vs-deregulation-as-the-pendulum-swings-a254863 (accessed August 30, 2013).

Larkin, Karen Y. "The History of Bank Deregulation." eHow.com. www.ehow.com/about_5413083_ history-bank-deregulation.html (accessed August 31, 2013).

Lister, Jonathan. "The Effects of Financial Deregulation." eHow.com. www.ehow.com/list_6708740_ effects-financial-deregulation.html (accessed August 31, 2013).

Sherman, Matthew. "A Short History of Financial Deregulation in the United States." The Center for Economic and Policy Research, July 2009. www.openthegovernment.org/sites/default/files/ otg/dereg-timeline-2009-07.pdf (accessed August 30, 2013).

What the Flock Were They Thinking? Straight, Not-So-Straight, and Crooked Preachers

"Aimee Semple McPherson." The Foursquare Church. www.foursquare.org/about/aimee_semple_ mcpherson (accessed August 26, 2013).

"Bishop Eddie Long Settlement Allegedly Cost $15 Million." *LA Late News*, June 1, 2011. news.lalate .com/2011/06/01/bishop-eddie-long-settlement-allegedly-cost-15-million/ (accessed August 26, 2013)

"Charlotte-Area Commissioner Caught in Prostitution Scandal Announces Resignation." *WSOCTV.com*, September 18, 2007. www.wsoctv.com/news/news/charlotte-area-commissioner-caught-in-prostitution/nGzQm/ (accessed August 26, 2013).

"Eddie Long Grants Ch. 2 First Interview Since Sex Allegations." *WSBTV.com*, January 27, 2011. www.wsbtv.com/news/26641142/detail.html (accessed August 26, 2013).

"Evangelical Group Leader Quits Post: The Rev. Ted Haggard Denies Charge That He Paid Man to Have Sex." *Albany Times Union*, November 3, 2006.

"Evangelical Leader Quits, Denies Male Escort's Allegations." *CNN.com*, November 2, 2006. www.cnn.com/2006/US/11/02/haggard.allegations/ (accessed August 26, 2013).

"George Rekers, Anti-Gay Activist, Caught with Male Escort 'Rentboy.'" *Huffington Post*, July 5, 2010. www.huffingtonpost.com/2010/05/05/george-rekers-anti-gay-ac_n_565142.html (accessed August 26, 2013).

"Kidnapping of Aimee Semple McPherson." University of Southern California. www.usc.edu/libraries/archives/la/scandals/aimee.html (accessed August 26, 2013).

"The 25 Most Influential Evangelicals in America: Ted Haggard." *TIME.com*, February 7, 2005. www.time.com/time/specials/packages/article/0,28804,1993235_1993243_1993280,00.html (accessed August 26, 2013).

Dees, Diane E. "God Does A Flip-Flop—Tells Richard Roberts To Resign From ORU." *Mother Jones*, November 28, 2007. www.motherjones.com/mojo/2007/11/god-does-flip-flop-tells-richard-roberts-resign-oru (accessed August 26, 2013).

Harris, Art. "$$$ and Sins: Jim Bakker's Case Hits Court; In Charlotte, a Sordid Saga Nears Its Spicy Conclusion." *Washington Post*, August 22, 1989.

Harris, Art. "Bakker Convicted On All 24 Fraud, Conspiracy Counts; Televangelist Out on Bond Until Oct. 24 Sentencing." *Washington Post*, October 6, 1989.

Saperstein, Saundra. "Jimmy Swaggart Ministries Is Accountable." *Washington Post*, June 15, 1987.

Test-Drive the Luxurious New Ford Lemon Sucker

"A Great Big Edsel in the Sky." *Insight on the News*, June 21, 1999.

"Cautionary Tale of the Ford Edsel Still Holds Lessons." *Australasian Business Intelligence*, September 23, 2007.

"Happy Birthday Edsel, America's Favorite Flop." *Seattle Post-Intelligencer*, August 1, 1997.

Bonsall, Thomas E. *Disaster in Dearborn: The Story of the Edsel.* Stanford, CA: Stanford General Books, 2002.

Neil, Dan. "The 50 Worst Cars of All Time: 1958 Ford Edsel." *TIME.com*. www.time.com/time/specials/2007/article/0,28804,1658545_1657867_1657781,00.html (accessed August 19, 2013).

I Can Stop This Train—and I'm Not Just Yanking Your Chain

"15 Caught On Chain Pulling Charges." *Times of India*, August 11, 2011. articles.timesofindia.indiatimes.com/2011-08-11/varanasi/29875904_1_unauthorised-chain-aurihar-varanasi-division (accessed August 26, 2013).

"Emergency Brake (Train)." Wikipedia. en.wikipedia.org/wiki/Chain_pulling (accessed August 26, 2013).

Mehta, Manthan K. "Chain-Pulling Delays 25 Central Railway Trains Every Day." *Times of India*, May 15, 2013. articles.timesofindia.indiatimes.com/2013-05-15/mumbai/39281042_1_suburban-train-senior-cr-official-long-distance-trains (accessed August 26, 2013).

Oh, the Stupidity!

"Hindenburg (LZ-129)." Navy Lakehurst Historical Society. www.nlhs.com/hindenburg.htm (accessed August 26, 2013).

DiChristina, Mariette. "What Really Downed the Hindenburg; Retired NASA Engineer Addison Bain Claims He Has Found the Fatal Flaw." *Popular Science*, November 1, 1997.

Duggan, John. *LZ 129 Hindenburg: The Complete Story*. Ickenham, UK: Zeppelin Study Group, 2002.

Goltz, Anna. *Hindenburg: Power, Myth, and the Rise of the Nazis*. Oxford: Oxford University Press, 2009.

Hoehling, Adolph A. *Who Destroyed the Hindenburg?* Boston: Little, Brown & Co, 1962.

Holy Schettino, How Did That Guy Become a Captain?

"5 Cruise Employees Convicted in *Costa Concordia* Shipwreck." *CBSNews.com*, July 20, 2013. www.cbsnews.com/8301-202_162-57594698/5-cruise-employees-convicted-in-costa-concordia-shipwreck/ (accessed August 26, 2013).

Borghese, Livia. "Italian Cruise Ship Captain Freed from House Arrest." *CNN.com*, July 6, 2012. articles.cnn.com/2012-07-05/world/world_europe_italy-cruise-ship-captain_1_house-arrest-cruise-liner-italian-island?_s=PM:EUROPE (accessed August 26, 2013).

Jones, Gavin, and Antonio Denti. "Stricken Italian Liner Shifts, 29 People Missing." *Reuters.com*, January 16, 2012. www.reuters.com/article/2012/01/16/us-italy-ship-idUSTRE80D08220120116 (accessed August 26, 2013).

Piangiani, Gaia, and Alan Cowell. "More Bodies Found on Ship, as Transcripts Reveal Rebuke to Captain." *New York Times*, January 17, 2012. www.nytimes.com/2012/01/18/world/europe/rescuers-search-for-survivors-in-italian-cruise-ship-accident.html (accessed August 26, 2013).

Squires, Nick. "I'm Not the Captain's Lover: *Costa Concordia* Mystery Woman Speaks Out." *London Telegraph*, January 20, 2012. www.telegraph.co.uk/news/worldnews/europe/italy/9027973/Im-not-the-captains-lover-Costa-Concordia-mystery-woman-speaks-out.html (accessed August 26, 2013).

Winfield, Nicole. "Search Aboard the *Costa Concordia* Resumes."*U-T San Diego*, January 20, 2012. www.utsandiego.com/news/2012/Jan/20/search-aboard-the-costa-concordia-resumes/ (accessed August 25, 2013).

They Sing the Body Electric, Then Hummer a Different Tune

"Who Killed the Electric Car?" *PBS.org*. www.pbs.org/now/shows/223/ (accessed August 26, 2013).

"Zero Emission Vehicle (ZEV) Program." California Environmental Protection Agency, Air Resources Board. www.arb.ca.gov/msprog/zevprog/zevprog.htm (accessed August 26, 2013).

Loveday, Eric. "2009 Hummer H3—Review." Green Car Reports, May 29, 2009. www.greencarreports.com/review/1021088_review-100-mpg-raser-hummer-h3-plug-in (accessed August 26, 2013).

Tesla Motors. www.teslamotors.com/ (accessed August 26, 2013).

Who Killed the Electric Car?—the Documentary. DVD. Directed by Chris Paine. Worldwide: Sony Pictures Home Entertainment, 2006.

A Horseless Carriage of a Different Color?

Ford, Henry, and Samuel Crowther. *My Life and Work.* Garden City, NY: Doubleday, Page & Co., 1922.

"The Life of Henry Ford." The Henry Ford Museum. www.hfmgv.org/exhibits/hf/ (accessed August 29, 2013).

Uncool at Any Speed

"Nader v. General Motors Corp." CaseBriefs.com. www.casebriefs.com/blog/law/torts/torts-keyed-to-epstein/privacy/nader-v-general-motors-corp/ (accessed August 30, 2013).

"This Day in History: Unsafe at Any Speed Hits Bookstores." History.com. www.history.com/this-day-in-history/unsafe-at-any-speed-hits-bookstores (accessed August 30, 2013).

"Unsafe at Any Speed." Wikipedia. en.wikipedia.org/wiki/Unsafe_at_Any_Speed (accessed August 30, 2013).

Nader, Ralph. *Unsafe at Any Speed: The Designed-in Dangers of the American Automobile.* New York: Grossman, 1965.

Blind Ambition Meets Highway Robbery

"Patent US3351836: Windshield Wiper System with Intermittent Operation." U.S. Patent Office. www.google.com/patents?id=_qVQAAAAEBAJ&printsec=abstract&zoom=4#v=onepage&q&f=false (accessed September 1, 2013).

"Robert Kearns, 77, Inventor of Intermittent Wipers, Dies." *New York Times,* February 26, 2005. www.nytimes.com/2005/02/26/obituaries/26kearns.html?_r=0 (accessed September 1, 2013).

"Robert W. Kearns v. Chrysler Corporation and American Motors ." Bulk.Resource.org. https://bulk.resource.org/courts.gov/c/F3/32/32.F3d.1541.93-1470.93-1450.html (accessed August 31, 2013).

Flash of Genius. Film. Directed by Marc Abraham. Universal City, CA: Universal Studios Home Entertainment, 2009.

Gross, Ken. "Wiper Man Robert Kearns Won His Patent Fight with Ford, but That Didn't Mean He Was Out of the Woods." *People.com,* August 6, 1990. www.people.com/people/archive/article/0,,20118404,00.html (accessed September 1, 2013).

Johnson, Reed. "The Cantankerous Man Behind the Wipers." *Los Angeles Times,* October 3, 2008. articles.latimes.com/2008/oct/03/entertainment/et-kearns3 (accessed September 1, 2013).

Schudel, Matt. "Accomplished, Frustrated Inventor Dies." *Washington Post,* February 26, 2005. www.washingtonpost.com/wp-dyn/articles/A54564-2005Feb25.html (accessed September 1, 2013).

The *Titanic*: One Bad Idea Begets Four Others

"History of the Titanic." Titanic Facts. www.titanic-facts.com/history-of-titanic.html (accessed September 1, 2013).

"Sinking of the RMS *Titanic*." Wikipedia. en.wikipedia.org/wiki/Sinking_of_the_RMS_Titanic (accessed September 1, 2013).

Aldridge, Rebecca. *The Sinking of the Titanic*. New York: Chelsea House, 2008.

Bassett, Vicki. "Titanic: Causes and Effects of the Rapid Sinking." Undergraduate Engineering Review. www.writing.eng.vt.edu/uer/bassett.html (accessed September 1, 2013).

Weir, Stephen. *Encyclopedia Idiotica: History's Worst Decisions and the People Who Made Them*. Hauppauge, NY: Barron's, 2005.

Mr. Cane Toad's Wild Rise

"Australia's Cane Toads." *NPR.org*, April 24, 2000. www.npr.org/programs/re/archivesdate/2000/apr/000424.canetoads.html (accessed August 21, 2013).

"Cane Toads." *National Geographic*. video.nationalgeographic.com/video/animals/amphibians-animals/frogs-and-toads/toad_cane/ (accessed August 21, 2013).

"Cane Toads: Toxic toads leap across Australia." National Geographic Education. education.nationalgeographic.com/education/media/cane-toads/?ar_a=1 (accessed August 21, 2013).

"Invasive Species: Animals–Cane Toad (Rhinella Marina)." National Invasive Species Information Center. www.invasivespeciesinfo.gov/animals/canetoad.shtml (accessed August 21, 2013).

Peter, Michael. "Beer Bounty for Cane Toads." *Australian*, February 26, 2007. www.theaustralian.com.au/news/beer-bounty-for-cane-toads/story-0-1111113058424 (accessed August 21, 2013).

Silverman, Art. "Cane Toads As Means To Riches." *NPR.org*, March 27, 2009. www.npr.org/templates/story/story.php?storyId=102448050 (accessed August 21, 2013).

These Dudes Must Have Been High When They Made This Weed Deal

"Genetically Modified Crops: European Farming at Risk." Friends of the Earth International, March 18, 2013. www.foei.org/en/blog/genetically-modified-crops-european-farming-at-risk (accessed August 25, 2013).

"Monsanto Canada Inc. v. Schmeiser." Wikipedia. en.wikipedia.org/wiki/Monsanto_Canada_Inc._v._Schmeiser (accessed August 25, 2013).

Chait, Jennifer. "Organic Farmers File Suit Against Monsanto Co. Challenging Patents on GE Seed." About.com, March 31, 2011. organic.about.com/b/2011/03/31/organic-farmers-file-suit-against-monsanto-co-challenging-patents-on-ge-seed.htm (accessed August 25, 2013).

Mercola, Joseph. "Finally…Solo Farmer Fights Monsanto and Wins." Mercola.com, December 25, 2011. articles.mercola.com/sites/articles/archive/2011/12/25/percy-schmeiser-farmer-who-beat-monsanto.aspx (accessed August 25, 2013).

Richardson, Jill. "Research Shows That Monsanto's Big Claims for GMO Food Are Probably Wrong." Alternet.org, June 25, 2013. www.alternet.org/food/why-monsanto-wrong-about-gm-crop-promises (accessed August 25, 2013).

Oilpocalypse Now

"BP Adds $847M to Deepwater Horizon Costs." *Guardian*, July 31, 2012. www.guardian.co.uk/business/2012/jul/31/deepwater-horizon-bp-847m-dollars (accessed August 18, 2013).

"Gulf Coast Oil Spill: Does Federal Government Share Responsibility?" *States News Service (Washington)*, May 12, 2010.

Baird, Julia. "Oil's Shame in Africa." *Newsweek*, July 26, 2010.

Fowler, Tom. "BP: Nearly All of $20 Billion Oil Spill Fund Gone" *Wall Street Journal*, July 31, 2013. live.wsj.com/video/bp-nearly-all-of-20-billion-oilspill-fund-gone/D33A15C6-B6A3-4C48-B3CD-CAFCAAA6591D.html?KEYWORDS=deepwater+horizon#!D33A15C6-B6A3-4C48-B3CD-CAFCAAA6591D (accessed August 18, 2013).

Fowler, Tom. "BP's New Move in Battle over Deepwater Horizon Damages." *Wall Street Journal*, August 7, 2013. blogs.wsj.com/riskandcompliance/2013/08/07/bps-new-move-in-battle-over-deepwater-horizon-damages/?KEYWORDS=deepwater+horizon (accessed August 18, 2013).

Smith, Sandy. "Where Was BP's Credit Check?? The Oil Spill in the Gulf of Mexico Is Another Grim Reminder That Due Diligence on the Part of Government Agencies Is Necessary When Lives and the Environment Are at Stake." *EHS Today*, June 1, 2010.

Steinzor, Rena. "Deepwater Horizon Spill Commission Waivers on Self-Regulation, Endorses Wrong-Headed British 'Safety Cases' System." *Huffington Post*, January 11, 2011. www.huffingtonpost.com/rena-steinzor/deepwater-horizon-spill-c_b_807471.html (accessed August 17, 2013).

Attack of the Frankenfish

"Environmental Damage from Escaped Farmed Salmon." Pure Salmon Campaign. www.puresalmon.org/escapes.html (accessed August 25, 2013).

"The Emerging Scientific Debate on Frankenfish." Organic Consumers Association. www.organicconsumers.org/ge/gmfish.cfm (accessed August 25, 2013).

Avila, Jim, and Serena Marshall. "AquaBounty Hoping to Serve DNA-Altered Salmon on US Plates." *ABCNews.com*, December 4, 2012. abcnews.go.com/Technology/aquabounty-hoping-serve-dna-altered-salmon-us-plates/story?id=17878998 (accessed August 25, 2013).

Blumenthal, Les. "Giant Salmon a Scary Prospect: Genetic Engineering Prompts Worries about 'Frankenfish.'" *News Tribune*, August 21, 2000. www.mindfully.org/GE/Giant-Salmon.htm (accessed August 25, 2013).

Fleming, Ian A. et al. "Lifetime Success and Interactions of Farm Salmon Invading a Native Population." *Proceedings of the Royal Society of London* 267, no. 1452 (August 2000): 1517-1523. rspb.royalsocietypublishing.org/content/267/1452/1517.short (accessed August 25, 2013).

Lochner, Mary. "Who's Afraid of Frankenfish?" *Anchorage Press News*, January 24, 2013. www.anchoragepress.com/news/who-s-afraid-of-frankenfish/article_82687380-6668-11e2-91f7-0019bb2963f4.html (accessed August 25, 2013).

The Pesticide That Commits Homicide

"DDT—A Brief History and Status." U.S. Environmental Protection Agency. www.epa.gov/pesticides/factsheets/chemicals/ddt-brief-history-status.htm (accessed August 25, 2013).

Carson, Rachel. *Silent Spring*. Boston: Houghton Mifflin, 1962.

Koehn, Nancy F. "From Calm Leadership, Lasting Change." *New York Times*, October 27, 2012. www.nytimes.com/2012/10/28/business/rachel-carsons-lessons-50-years-after-silent-spring.html?pagewanted=all (accessed August 25, 2013).

Bad Ideas Gone Good

"Art Fry and Spencer Silver: Post-It Notes." Massachusetts Institute of Technology. web.mit.edu/invent/iow/frysilver.html (accessed August 25, 2013).

"Books about Louis Braille and His Invention." U.S. Library of Congress. www.loc.gov/nls/bibliographies/minibibs/louisbraille.html (accessed August 21, 2013).

"Famous Mayflower Descendants." MayflowerHistory.com. mayflowerhistory.com/famous-descendants/ (accessed August 21, 2013).

"Fleming Discovers Penicillin." *PBS.org*. www.pbs.org/wgbh/aso/databank/entries/dm28pe.html (accessed August 25, 2013).

"History & Heritage." Levi's. us.levi.com/shop/index.jsp?categoryId=18816896 (accessed August 25, 2013).

"The History of Post-It." 3M Company. www.post-it.com/wps/portal/3M/en_US/Post_It/Global/About/History/ (accessed August 25, 2013).

Bellis, Mary. "The History of Penicillin." About.com. inventors.about.com/od/pstartinventions/a/Penicillin.htm (accessed August 25, 2013).

Bickel, Lennard. *Triumph Over Darkness: The Life of Louis Braille*. Leicester, UK: Ulverscroft, 1988.

Downey, Lynn. "Levi Strauss: A Short Biography." Levi Strauss & Co. www.levistrauss.com/sites/default/files/librarydocument/2010/4/History_Levi_Strauss_Biography.pdf (accessed August 13, 1924).

Jones, Charlotte Foltz, and John Brien. *Mistakes That Worked*. New York: Doubleday, 1991.

Kugelmass, J. Alvin. *Louis Braille: Windows for the Blind*. New York: Messner, 1972.

Parr, Jerry. "Secret Service Agent Jerry Parr's Account of the March 30, 1981 Assassination Attempt on President Ronald Reagan." Shapell Manuscript Foundation. www.shapell.org/manuscript.aspx?secret-service-agent-jerry-parr-on-reagan-assassination-attempt (accessed August 21, 2013).

White, Elizabeth Pearson, Edwin Wagner Coles, and Roberta Gilbert Bratti. *John Howland of the Mayflower*. Camden, ME: Picton Press, 1990.

Wilber, Del Quentin. *Rawhide Down: The Near Assassination of Ronald Reagan*. New York: Henry Holt and Co., 2011.

INDEX

MICHAEL N. SMITH AND ERIC KASUM

MICHAEL N. SMITH AND ERIC KASUM

MICHAEL N. SMITH AND ERIC KASUM